OCR
LATIN
ANTHOLOGY
for GCSE

TEACHER'S HANDBOOK

Peter McDonald
Margaret Widdess

OCR
RECOGNISING ACHIEVEMENT
OXFORD
UNIVERSITY PRESS
Official Publisher Partnership

OXFORD
UNIVERSITY PRESS

Great Clarendon Street, Oxford OX2 6DP

Oxford University Press is a department of the
University of Oxford. It furthers the University's
objective of excellence in research, scholarship, and
education by publishing worldwide in

Oxford   New York

Auckland   Cape Town   Dar es Salaam   Hong Kong
Karachi   Kuala Lumpur   Madrid   Melbourne
Mexico City   Nairobi   New Delhi   Shanghai
Taipei   Toronto

With offices in

Argentina   Austria   Brazil   Chile   Czech Republic
France   Greece   Guatemala   Hungary   Italy
Japan   South Korea   Poland   Portugal   Singapore
Switzerland   Thailand   Turkey   Ukraine   Vietnam

Oxford is a registered trade mark of Oxford University
Press in the UK and in certain other countries

© Oxford University Press 2009

British Library Cataloguing in Publication Data

Data available

ISBN 978 019 832931 2

10 9 8 7 6 5 4 3 2 1

Printed in Great Britain by Bell & Bain, Glasgow

Acknowledgements
The authors are very grateful to a number of people
for their generous assistance and encouragement: Liz
Lucas (OUP), our copy-editor Sarah Newton, Anna Davey
(OCR), James Morwood for kind permisssion to use his
biographies of Latin authors; Richard Widdess; all who
read the material and made suggestions, especially
Stephen Spowart, Tim Hands, Steffan Griffiths, Isobel
Hurst and Gillian Mead. We are also indebted to our
colleagues and pupils over the years and to our own
teachers who introduced us to Latin literature.

Map © Oxford University Press

© **Mixed Sources**
Product group from well-managed
forests and other controlled sources
www.fsc.org Cert no. TT-COC-002769
© 1996 Forest Stewardship Council
FSC

Contents

SECTION 1 Vice and virtue

SECTION 2 Family life and relationships

INTRODUCTION

This *Teacher's Handbook* accompanies the *OCR Latin Anthology for GCSE* and its audio CD, which provide a basis for studying literature options to be examined in the new Latin GCSE from OCR for first examination in 2010. It aims to support teachers in their work on the literature set texts, especially those colleagues who are perhaps teaching Latin literature for the first time and those who are not necessarily subject specialists. We hope too that teachers will find within this *Handbook* ideas for further stimulus for those pupils who are already experienced in reading Latin.

The *Handbook*, like the *Anthology* (Students' Book), cannot be exhaustive, and does not provide all the answers. Rather we hope that it will help provide a way into the texts and some ideas for arriving at meaning, as well as some suggestions for teaching and learning. The style and layout varies from section to section reflecting the nature of the texts and different approaches. However, on each extract we have endeavoured to provide some general discussion including support in answering the questions which accompany the student text, and some remarks on linguistic and stylistic features, as well as details on proper names, and suggestions for further reading or comparative analysis.

Specific examination guidance and sample assessment materials can be found on the OCR website at **www.ocr.org.uk/qualifications/gcsefor2009/ latin/index.html**.

For those colleagues teaching Latin literature for the first time for an examination—some ideas

- The *Anthology* has plentiful glossing printed by the side of the texts, but you may need to supplement that, depending on the ability level of your students.
- Place the text in its context, but keep any introduction on biographical details brief, perhaps using the short biographies on the Latin writers provided in the *Anthology* (Students' Book pp. 154–155).

- Read the text to your students. Readings of the verse sections are on the audio CD.
- Work through the text with the students in class, arriving at either a collective translation—or ask them to do a write-up of a short section for homework (which is then marked or checked).
- Ask students to prepare a section, as individuals, pairs or at home, although probably not more than ten lines at a time. It can be useful to divide portions up between students, but it should be borne in mind that they will all need to know all of an examination text.
- Once the translation is known, ask regular comprehension questions.
- Discuss and analyse the text and the story, or the point of a poem. Some ideas are supplied in the Students' Book as well as in this *Handbook*.
- Students do need to know how to translate the text and which word means what.
- A regular summary of what's going on, provided either by teacher or student, is a useful learning tool, and should, in the case of an examination text, be supplemented by regular testing of the translation and how it fits together.
- Explore the style of the text, looking for alliteration (but only where it means something), repetition of words, position of words, choice of vocabulary, and possibly metre (although the latter is perhaps best left to a later stage).
- Introduce a few basic rhetorical/stylistic terms—there are plentiful definitions available on the Internet.
- For longer stories, a cartoon storyboard version of the text may prove useful.
- Aim at looking at overarching themes in any extract or combination of extracts, as well as how an author develops or emphasises any one particular feature in a passage. Some of these are identified in this *Handbook*.
- Emphasise that any revision needs to use both the Latin text and your translation!

There is no one recommended translation—part of the joy of teaching Latin literature is the whole process of arriving at meaning. Students should have a correct, checked, version that is close to the Latin. Frequently such resources are available via the OCR Classics e-community.

The 'Further reading' sections include those works which we have consulted or which might be useful for reference, as well as some books recommended for use by or with students. However, our aim has been to supply in this *Handbook* as much basic information as is necessary to understand the texts and guide students through them.

There are, of course, many approaches to the teaching of literature and below are some additional approaches, which you may wish to use to vary the procedure of translation and interpretation or for revision.

- 'Fill the gap': give a passage in translation with key words omitted, so that they have to be found, translated and supplied.
- Give alternative translations of key words/phrases for the correct one to be identified. Include variations of tense or case or number to ensure close reading.

- Content, descriptive passages or key nouns can be reinforced by students adding sound effects as they read aloud or by changing colour or font size appropriately as they type (e.g. *iratus* in red or *INGENS*).
- Draw up a series of 'true or false' statements in English to be checked from the Latin.

A note on the texts used

The text used throughout is the Oxford Classical Text, with some very occasional emendation. In 'Ever-changing love' (section 2.2d Family life and relationships—Catullus 51), the conjecture *vocis in ore* has been used for the lacuna.

In section 3 Passions and poisons and section 6 Prophecies and Portents the text used for the extracts from Ovid's *Heroides*, Suetonius' *Divine Julius* and Lucan's *Civil War* are the same as those of The Latin Library (**www.thelatinlibrary.com**).

The passages on 'Marital conflict' (section 5.4 Conquest and conflict—Cicero *Ad Atticum* 5.3) contain one textual change which is used by Balme and Morwood in *On the Margin*.

VERSE READINGS ON THE AUDIO CD

The verse readings were done by David Langslow, Ian McAuslan, James Morwood and Philomen Probert. We have aimed to follow the principles laid down in W. S. Allen's *Vox Latina* (2nd edn, revised reprint, Cambridge, 1989). Further valuable guidance can be found in his *Accent and Rhythm: Prosodic Features of Latin and Greek: A Study in Theory and Reconstruction* (Cambridge, 1973) and *The Blackwell History of the Latin Language* (Blackwell, 2007) by James Clackson and Geoffrey Horrocks. J. N. Adams's *The Regional Diversification of Latin: 200 BC–AD 600* (Cambridge, 2007) is a monumental and lucid account of the evidence for regional variation in spoken as well as written Latin in different parts of the empire and in different periods.

It is of course often difficult or impossible to be definitive about the way even upper-class inhabitants of Rome pronounced their language two thousand years ago. I attended Sidney Allen's lectures on the subject, delivered when he was working on *Vox Latina*, and remember his saying that, if he could be transported back to ancient Rome in a time machine, he thought the Romans would find his way of speaking Latin decidedly peculiar but would probably just about understand him! We have deliberately avoided uniformity in our procedures in a number of respects. We have adopted different approaches, for example, to the pronunciation of *h*, to the nasalisation of the vowel before *m*s and *n*s, and to elision (though we have elided short vowels except in special cases, e.g. when there is good reason to pause). We would hope that, the occasional slip apart, each of us could adduce justifications for what we have done. You may wish to get your students to experiment with the various approaches and see which they find the most sympathetic. Perhaps most importantly, we have all tried to avoid emphasising the rhythm of the verse (the ictus) and instead to give each word its natural spoken stress, according to the 'Law of the Penultimate Syllable' (viz., that if this is long, it is stressed, while if it is short and if the word has more than two syllables, the stress falls on the antepenultimate syllable). Philomen Probert has written an illuminating article on where to place the stress when an enclitic (most frequently *–que*) is added to the end of a word (go to **www.ling-phil.ox.ac.uk/download/OWP2002. pdf** and type 'On the prosody of Latin enclitics' in Find).

Since every student will have a copy of the audio CD, we very much hope that teachers will build its use into homework assignments and projects. If a passage is being prepared or revised, students can be asked to listen to it and comment on how this affects their reactions to it. It is our strong conviction that learning through the ear is as valuable and rewarding as learning through the eye, and of course Latin poetry was intended to be read out loud. When students are asked in question 2 on the first passage in the book, 'What features of Niobe's speech make it forceful?' a significant part of the answer should surely concern itself with the way it sounds. In addition, when reading a passage we almost inevitably adopt an interpretative stance. Students may dissent from the line we have taken and this could lead to stimulating discussion. Above all, of course, we hope that immersion in our readings will fire students with a passion for reading Latin aloud themselves. If this happens, it will enhance their Latin studies immeasurably.

James Morwood
Wadham College, Oxford

AUDIO CD TRACKLIST

1 Introduction

SECTION 1 VICE AND VIRTUE

1.1 Niobe's pride brings about her downfall

2 1.1 lines 1–19
3 1.1 lines 20–42
4 1.1 lines 43–57
5 1.1 lines 58–75
6 **1.2 The Elysian Fields, resting place of the virtuous**
7 **1.3 A hard-working wife**
8 **1.4 Different standards for men and women**

SECTION 2 FAMILY LIFE AND RELATIONSHIPS

2.1 Grief at parting

9 2.1 lines 1–34
10 2.1 lines 35–59
2.2 Love and Loss
11 2.2a farewell to a brother
12 2.2b Rejection in love
13 2.2c Jealousy takes over
14 2.2d Ever-changing love
15 **2.3 Sulpicia discovers love**
16 **2.4 Love for a young man**

SECTION 3 PASSIONS AND POISONS

3.3 A snake's poison stirs passion

17 3.3 lines 1–18
18 3.3 lines 19–32
3.4 Medea's impassioned plea
19 3.4 lines 1–24
20 3.4 lines 25–54
21 **3.5 Catullus struggles with love**
22 **3.6 Passion fades**
23 **3.7 The passions of a ghostly fury**

SECTION 4 LAND AND SEA

4.4 A traveller's tale

24 4.4 lines 1–9
25 4.4 lines 10–24
26 4.4 lines 25–34
27 4.4 lines 35–46
28 4.4 lines 47–57
29 4.4 lines 58–64
30 4.4 lines 65–72
4.5 Storm at sea
31 4.5 lines 1–11
32 4.5 lines 12–21
33 4.5 lines 22–32
34 4.5 lines 33–43
35 **4.6 The ship of state in troubled waters**

SECTION 5 CONFLICT AND CONQUEST

5.5 Atalanta meets her match

36 5.5 lines 1–28
37 5.5 lines 29–36
38 5.5 lines 37–59
39 5.5 lines 60–79
5.6 Advice for would-be lovers
40 5.6 lines 1–20
41 5.6 lines 21–58

SECTION 6 PROPHECIES AND PORTENTS

42 **6.4 Caesar crosses the Rubicon**
43 **6.5 Praying for profit**
44 **6.6 A sign from heaven**
6.7 The shield of Aeneas
45 6.7 lines 1–22
46 6.7 lines 23–65
47 6.7 lines 66–80
48 6.7 lines 81–83

METRE

While an appreciation of Latin poets' use of rhythm is expected for the OCR GCSE in Latin, detailed knowledge of prosody and scansion is *not* required. It is hoped that with the help of the following notes teachers will guide students to an awareness of metre in their study of Latin poetry and in their use of the readings on the audio CD provided with the Students' Book.

These notes also aim to provide enough information for those with the time and the interest to tackle the scansion of hexameters and elegiacs. More specialised descriptions and analysis of metres can be found in commentaries on the Latin poets.

Latin poetry is composed so that the words form metrical patterns comprising feet made up of long (marked ˉ) and/or short (marked ˘) syllables. In the examples below the end of each foot is marked with a single vertical stroke (|). Long syllables include naturally long vowels or diphthongs, or vowels followed by some combinations of consonants. Final vowels or syllables ending in a vowel plus –m are elided before vowels and before words beginning with *h*. Elisions are indicated in the examples below by ‿. In most metres there is a metrical break in the course of the line, and in some metres the position of this can vary. (In the examples below these breaks are indicated (||) only in hexameters and elegiacs.)

Additional notes

- Usually two consonants following a short vowel make the syllable long, but there are occasional exceptions.
- The metrical break in the line is called the *caesura* ('cutting').
- In many cases the final syllable in a line can be long or short, but in practice this does not affect the rhythm of the metre. In the metrical patterns given below, this 'doubtful' (*anceps*) syllable is marked ˣ.
- There may be irregularities in scansion where Greek names occur.

Variations in metre can convey rhythms appropriate to the meaning or the mood of a line. Unusual metrical effects can be used for emphasis. Some examples of striking metrical effects are discussed in the *Notes on text* sections included in this book for each passage in the *Anthology*.

Where poets such as Horace and Catullus use Greek lyric metres, they are indicating that they are following the genre of Sappho, Alcaeus and Archilochus.

As students listen to the audio CD, they can form an impression of the metres. When they are becoming familiar with the text, they might try reading the more common metres such as hexameters and elegiacs with the CD and on their own. As the final feet of lines tend to be unchanging, they can begin by identifying those and joining in with them as they are read.

1. **Dactylic hexameters**, most common in long poems such as epic and satire where the flexibility of the line's pattern provides variety. The following examples show how the line may consist of any combination of dactyls ˉ ˘ ˘ and spondees ˉ ˉ, or almost entirely of either dactyls or spondees, *except* that the last two feet are almost always a dactyl and a spondee:

$$\bar{\ }\,\breve{\ }\,\breve{\ }\mid\bar{\ }\,\bar{\ }\mid\bar{\ }\mid\mid\breve{\ }\,\breve{\ }\mid\bar{\ }\,\bar{\ }\mid\bar{\ }\,\breve{\ }\,\breve{\ }\mid\bar{\ }\,^{x}$$
$$\bar{\ }\,\bar{\ }\mid\bar{\ }\,\breve{\ }\,\breve{\ }\mid\bar{\ }\mid\mid\bar{\ }\mid\bar{\ }\,\bar{\ }\mid\bar{\ }\,\breve{\ }\,\breve{\ }\mid\bar{\ }\,^{x}$$
$$\bar{\ }\,\breve{\ }\,\breve{\ }\mid\bar{\ }\,\breve{\ }\,\breve{\ }\mid\bar{\ }\mid\mid\breve{\ }\,\breve{\ }\mid\bar{\ }\,\breve{\ }\,\breve{\ }\mid\bar{\ }\,\breve{\ }\,\breve{\ }\mid\bar{\ }\,^{x}$$

pārs pĕdĭ|būs plāu|dūnt || chŏrĕ|ās ēt | cārmĭnă | dīcūnt	1.2 line 8
cōntra‿āu|tēm mā|gnō || māē|rēntēm | cōrpŏrĕ | Nīlŭm	6.7 line 63
ēmĭcăt | ēt sūm|mām || cĕlĕ|rī pĕdĕ | lībăt hă|rēnăm	5.5 line 52
dāt lătŭs | īnsĕquĭ|tūr || cŭmŭ|lō prāe|rūptŭs ăq|uāe mōns	4.5 line 25

2. **Elegiacs or elegiac couplets**, regularly used in poetry expressing love or other strong personal feelings. The first line of the couplet is a hexameter, as above. The second line is a pentameter (five feet), consisting of the first part of a hexameter, repeated:

$$ - \smile \smile \mid - - \mid - \mid\mid \smile \smile \mid - - \mid - \smile \smile \mid - x $$
$$ - \smile \smile \mid - \smile \smile \mid - \mid\mid - \smile \smile \mid - \smile \smile \mid x $$

tū quŏquĕ | mātĕrĭ | ām || lōn | gō quī | quaerĭs ă | mōrī
āntĕ frĕ | quēns quō | sīt || dīscĕ || pŭ | ēllă lŏ | cō.   5.6 lines 6–7

āccĭpĕ | frātēr | nō || mūl | tūm mā | nāntĭă | flētū
ātque ‿ īn | pērpĕtŭ | ūm || frātĕr ă | ve ‿ ātquĕ vă | lē   2.2a lines 9–10

3. **Scazons or limping iambics.** The line consists of six iambs ($\smile -$), with spondees ($- -$) sometimes substituted, and the limping effect arises from the unexpected reversal of long and short syllables in the last foot. It is used by Catullus and Martial in poems of a bitter or satirical nature.

$$ \smile - \mid \smile - \mid \smile - \mid \smile - \mid \smile - \mid - x $$

mĭsēr | Cătūl | lĕ dē | sĭnās | ĭnē | ptīrĕ   2.2b line 1
āt tū | Cătūl | lĕ dē | stĭnā | tŭs ōb | dūrā   2.2b line 19

4. **Iambic senarii.** The metre regularly used for dialogue in the comedies of Plautus and Terence. Its basis is six iambic feet:

$$ \smile - \mid \smile - \mid \smile - \mid \smile - \mid \smile - \mid \smile - $$

The iamb may be a spondee ($- -$), and any of the long syllables in the line may be broken into short ones, giving a wide variety of patterns (which can include a foot of three short syllables, as in line 2 of the example below). The last foot is invariably an iamb, which preserves the iambic nature of the metre.

ēcā | stŏr lē | gĕ dū | rā vī | vōnt mŭlĭ | ĕrēs
mūltō | que ‿ īnī | quĭō | rĕ mĭsĕ | rāe quām | vĭrī   1.4 lines 1–2

The following **lyric metres** govern the whole verse, made up of two or three different metrical patterns in the lines. Feet have not been marked in the examples below.

5. **Alcaics.** The metre most frequently used by Horace in his *Odes*.

pārcūs dĕōrūm cūltŏr ĕt īnfrĕquēns
īnsānĭēntīs dūm săpĭēntĭāe
     cōnsūltŭs ērrō nūnc rĕtrōrsŭm
     vēlă dăre ‿ ātque ‿ ĭtĕrārĕ cūrsūs   6.6 lines 1–4

6. **Fourth Asclepiad**

ō nāvīs rĕfĕrēnt īn mărĕ tē nŏvī
flūctūs ō quĭd ăgīs fōrtĭtĕr ōccŭpā
     pōrtūm nōnnĕ vĭdēs ŭt
     nūdūm rēmĭgĭō lătŭs   4.6 lines 1–4

7. **Sapphics**

īllĕ mī pār ēssĕ dĕō vĭdētūr
īllĕ sī fās ēst sŭpĕrārĕ dīvōs
quī sĕdēns ādvērsŭs ĭdēntĭdēm tē
     spēctăt ĕt āudĭt   2.2c lines 1–4

8. **Second Sapphic strophe.** Horace uses this metre only once in his *Odes*: *Odes* 1.8, which occurs as passage 2.4 in the *Anthology*:

     Lȳdĭă dīc pĕr ōmnēs
hōc dĕōs vērē Sȳbărĭn cūr prŏpĕrēs ămāndō   2.4 lines 1–2

ILLUSTRATIONS

The pictures in the *Anthology* provide illustrations of different kinds for the texts to be studied.

- **Ancient artefacts**
  A number of reliefs, mosaics, statues, busts and coins, and photographs of buildings and places provide information on people and the context of Roman life in which the texts are set.

- **Later works of art**
  Paintings and other artefacts are evidence of the persistence of ancient Roman literature and knowledge of it as well as its reception and interpretation by later artists.

SECTION 1 Vice and virtue

SECTION 2 Family life and relationships

SECTION 3 Passions and poisons

Using the pictures

Teaching suggestions for use of the pictures.

- **As a stimulus**
  Examples:
  1 Cicero, p.21
    What kind of person do you think this is?
    Is there any way in which you can relate this portrait to the title page picture of section 2, The young Cicero reading, p. 29?

  2 Medea and Jason with their children, p. 69
    How does the composition of the picture show the family relationships?
    What sinister feature makes the picture different from a family portrait?

  3 Title page, 5 Conflict and conquest: Augustus as a triumphant general, p.103
    How does the statue express the idea of conquest?
    How might it be regarded by Rome's enemies?
    What other kinds of conquest are there?

- **Exploring the text**
  Examples:
  1 Street of the Tombs, Pompei, p.35
    How does the picture convey the melancholy and sense of loss of 2.2/2.6?

  2 Title page, 3 Passions and poisons: Medea mixes poison, p. 53
    Which parts of the story does this painting illustrate (in the background as well as the foreground)?
    How does the painter portray Medea?
    In what ways does Medea in this picture arouse sympathy or revulsion?

  3 Title page, 6 Prophecies and portents: Caesar and the Ides of March, p. 125
    Which characters from 6.3 are shown?
    How are the characters connected with portents of Caesar's death?
    How does Caesar show his attitude to the warnings he has been given?

  4 Title page, 4 Land and sea: Funerary Monument of M. Viriatius Zosimus, p. 77; and Three men in a boat, p.91
    Which parts of 'A traveller's tale' could these pictures illustrate?

  5 Coin celebrating Augustus' victory at Actium, p.148
    How effective is this coin as a way of communicating the news of the victory to the empire?

- **Later representations of the subject-matter of texts**
  Examples:
  1 Title page, Vice and virtue: Children of Niobe, p. 7
    Which parts of the story are shown here?
    How can you tell who the figures in the clouds are?
    What sense of the picture could you make if you didn't know the story in Ovid?
    Why might someone want to display a picture of this scene?
    What does this picture tell us about classics in the 17–18th centuries?

  2 Title page, 6 Prophecies and portents: Caesar and the Ides of March, p. 125
    See Exploring the text 3 above.
    Do you have to know what this picture is to consider it to be a good picture?

  3 Battle of Actium, p.148
    How does the artist show knowledge of Roman battles? (Compare the picture on p. 85.)

- **General questions**
  Many of the pictures lend themselves to general questions:

  What does this picture tell us about ... (ships, Roman dress, craftsmanship, decoration etc.)?

  What does this picture add to our understanding/appreciation of the text?

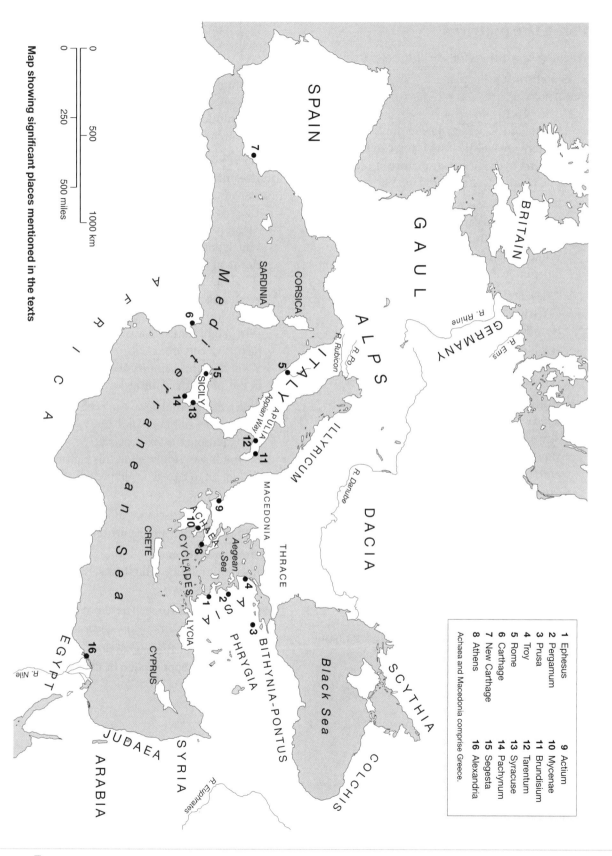

Map showing significant places mentioned in the texts

1 Ephesus	9 Actium
2 Pergamum	10 Mycenae
3 Prusa	11 Brundisium
4 Troy	12 Tarentum
5 Rome	13 Syracuse
6 Carthage	14 Pachynum
7 New Carthage	15 Segesta
8 Athens	16 Alexandria

Achaea and Macedonia comprise Greece.

1 VICE AND VIRTUE

Content overview

🔊 Verse

1. Niobe's pride brings about her downfall: Ovid *Metamorphoses*
2. The Elysian Fields, resting place of the virtuous: Virgil *Aeneid*
3. A hard-working wife: Virgil *Aeneid*
4. Different standards for men and women: Plautus *Mercator*

Prose

5. The corruption and cruelty of Verres and Cleomenes: Cicero *In Verrem*
6. The bravery of Mucius Scaevola and Cloelia: Livy *A History of Rome*

Themes in this section

Virtuous behaviour	2, 3, 4, 6
in men	2, 6
in women	3, 6
Indulging in vices	1, 4, 5
wicked women	1
wicked men	4, 5
Punishment and reward	1, 2, 5, 6
Divinity and the Underworld	1, 2, 3
Remembering the good	2, 6
Roman standards	4, 5, 6
Marital expectations	3, 4

🔊 1. Niobe's pride brings about her downfall—Ovid *Metamorphoses* 6.165–312 (abridged)

This dramatic tale of divine retribution allows students to work with an accessible mythological narrative whilst also seeing some of Ovid's subtle humour and playful moralising. Niobe becomes a ridiculous character in her pride, but it will be worth asking the question does she deserve such a horrific death for all of her children. Ovid typically does not hold back in his exaggeration, and she too will be metamorphosed into a 'weeping' rock (on Mt Sipylus) by the end of the episode.

Themes for exploration

- The character of Niobe
- The role of women
- Pride and other vices
- Revenge, retribution and punishment
- The role of the gods, and their relationships with human beings
- Ovidian exaggeration and subtlety—his light touch when dealing with grand themes

Metre—Hexameters

People and places

Niobe—Phrygian princess, married to Amphion of Thebes

Phrygia (Phrygius)—a kingdom situated in western central Turkey (Phrygian)

Latona—goddess and mother of Apollo and Diana (Phoebus and Phoebe); mother goddess of Lycia in western Turkey

Tantalus—father of Niobe; king of Sipylus, in Phrygia; fed his son Pelops to the gods, stealing ambrosia and nectar from them; later punished in the Underworld by not being able to reach food and drink

Pleiades—the seven daughters of Atlas and Pleione, who became first doves and then stars; no one can be certain who the mother of Niobe is—it may be Dione

Atlas—the Titan who supported the heavens, and grandfather of Niobe through her mother

Iuppiter—Jupiter, king of the gods and grandfather of Niobe through her father, Tantalus

Cadmus—founder of the city of Thebes. Some say Amphion, Niobe's husband, constructed the walls of the city of Thebes with his brother Zethus.

Cynthus—a mountain located on the island of Delos, where Latona gave birth to her children

Iuno—Juno, queen of the gods and wife of Jupiter

Notes on text

Lines 1–19

The character of Niobe is given a suitable build-up by use of the dramatic *ecce* and the use of the superlative in line **1**. The reader's focus is therefore appropriately on Niobe and she has clothing suitable for her status, but also for her character in line **2**. The pause in sense after *formosa* in line **3**, allows us to think that Ovid begrudges her the compliment, whilst also adding to the natural pause after her physical entrance. Ovid focuses on three parts of her upper body (line **4**), before telling us that her height gives her an added advantage (line **5**). Her questions before her explanation of her family tree convey her anger: the contrast between *auditos* and *visis* (line **6**) should be emphasised to students. Niobe considers herself a goddess on earth. The long list of 'big names' in her genealogy gives ample scope for exploration of the mythology of these characters. In lines **13–15**, Niobe's constant focus is herself, as witnessed by the personal pronouns. Her wealth is stressed in various ways—*in quamcumque … partem/immensae … opes* (**16–17**), and we are given further evidence that Niobe considers herself divine in lines **17–18**. In lines **18–19**, we reach the point of Niobe's boasts which will prove her downfall—that about her children. She even has the temerity to be smug about her sons- and daughters-in-law.

Lines 20–42

Niobe's confidence is evident from the outset of this passage with the simple numerical statement (**20–21**). This is rapidly reinforced by the short clauses, the questions and the first person verbs in lines **22–23**, and the wordplay on *multaque/multo*

plura in line **25** ensures that she becomes indeed a hostage to Fortune. The overconfidence is all too apparent with the imperative *fingite* (**26**), and by spelling out what she thinks can never happen, she almost challenges Latona to ensure that that is exactly what is brought about. After her haughty instructions to the other women, the *tacito murmure* (**32**) holds a multitude of meanings, as to whether their worship is willing or not. That some doubt is left in the mind of the reader automatically undermines Niobe's position.

Latona seethes and heads off to Delos, there to address her children, Apollo and Diana. In her speech she focuses on her role as a parent, and then her role as a goddess, imploring their help to ensure that worship continues at her altars. Various dramatic features of the speech include her declaration of *ego vestra parens* (**35**), the position of *arceor* in line **38**, and the direct appeal to her children (*o nati*: **38**). Not only has Niobe prevented worship of Latona but she has also insulted her, thereby slipping into the wicked ways of her father Tantalus.

Lines 43–57

This third scene is full of pathos, but at the same time we know that Niobe's pain is not nearly at its end. She is distraught as she leans over her sons' cold bodies, and bestows kisses upon them, before turning her bruised arms (from mournful self-harm) to the heavens (lines **43–45**). She directs her anger and suffering at Latona as if she knows that is its origin. Her repetition of the two imperatives *pascere* and *satia* (**46–48**) emphasises not only her anger but also her pleading. However in bringing back the topic of her speech to the basic numbers (**48**), Niobe reminds us of the fact that only her seven sons have died up until this point. She acknowledges Latona's victory in line **49** with two more imperatives, only to fall prey to boasting and pride once more, following her indignant question in line **50**.

Ovid presents us with an auditory picture very cleverly as Niobe finishes speaking. Not only are we allowed to hear the twang of the bowstring, but by focusing on the bow, the operator of the bow is removed from the picture, and it is as much an unseen hand for us as it is for Niobe (line **52**). The focus remains briefly on the unrepentant Niobe with the use of *unam* (**53**) and *illa* (**54**), as well as the brevity of the first clause of line **54**. Amidst the signs of mourning it moves to her daughters in line **55**, and to one in particular by the end of the passage. It is particularly poignant that she is still tending to her brother's body as she meets her end.

Lines 58–75

With use of *haec* and *illa*, Ovid gives intimate detail of the death of Niobe's daughters, moving from one to another as they are picked off (lines **58–59**), particularly drawing the reader's attention with *videres* (**59**). As we move back to the numbers of the dead, it is an automatic sign for Niobe's panic now, and her endeavours to shield her youngest daughter are stressed by the repetition of *toto/tota*, and the use of chiasmus ('*unam minimamque ... minimam posco' clamavit 'et unam*') and repetition in her pleading to leave the youngest and now only daughter (lines **61–63**). After she sits down, and Ovid presents us with a catalogue of the dead (line **65**), the metamorphosis begins in line **66**. The various stages of her transformation are listed, and typically of Ovid, she retains a feature (weeping) from her human existence.

Further teaching suggestions

- 🔊 Listen to the audio CD (tracks 2–5). How does the sound and pace of the story affect our reactions to Niobe?
- List the camera shots for a film of the story.
- Use the story as a springboard for a balloon debate involving students in choosing characters from classical mythology and their various claims to superiority.

Further reading

- Translations of Ovid's *Metamorphoses* (widely available).
- Brown, Sarah Annes, *Ovid Myth and Metamorphosis*, Ancients in Action (Bristol: Bristol Classical Press, 2005).
- Hardie, Philip (ed.), *The Cambridge Companion to Ovid* (Cambridge: Cambridge University Press, 2002).
- The paintings of the myth by Bloemart and Lemonnier

🔊 2. The Elysian Fields, resting place of the virtuous— Virgil *Aeneid* 6.637–665

This brief extract from Book 6 of Virgil's *Aeneid* outlines the happy times awaiting those who have been virtuous in the world of human beings. Aeneas is on a quest to find his father Anchises in the Underworld.

Themes for exploration

- Modern and ancient concepts of virtue and reward
- Modern and ancient ideas of the afterlife
- The role of the hero

Metre—Hexameters

People and places

Troia—Troy

Eridanus—for Virgil, a river of the Underworld, although others have it as a river in northern Europe, possibly the Po

Other references are explained in the Students' Book.

Notes on text

In the first five lines of the passage, Virgil sets a very pleasant scene indeed, using the balanced, chiastic phrasing of *locos ... virecta*, and *l* alliteration as well as some soft sibilance in lines **2** and **3**. We may take the internal rhyming of *fortunatorum nemorum* as creating an echoing sound suggesting open space. The *l* alliteration continues into line **4**, and the neat chiasmus of line **5** (*solemque suum, sua sidera*), adds to the sense of a separate little world for those who have behaved virtuously. Their activities in lines **6–8** suggest a repeat of those happy activities in which they indulged whilst on earth, and Virgil's portrayal of the dancing is made most vivid in line **8** with some *p* alliteration.

In line **9** the focus switches to Orpheus, followed by a grand introduction for the list of Trojan heroes in lines **12–13**, with a reverential adjective at every stage. Lines **15–19** make it clear that they too indulge in such activities as was their wont during their human existence, although here, there is no need for warfare—their chariots are empty, their spears fixed in the ground and the horses can graze away to their hearts content. In line **20**, *conspicit* reminds us that it is Aeneas viewing this scene, whilst the *ecce* draws the reader's eye off to the new sphere which Aeneas has discovered. From the spirits, Virgil draws us back once more to their natural surroundings, and another reminder of that pleasant environment. The final six lines list others who have lived virtuously in similarly reverential terms. They are marked out by their white headbands.

Further teaching suggestions

- Look at the rest of *Aeneid* 6 with your class considering the punishments which are set for those who have been wicked during their lives on earth.
- Discuss varying ideas of life after death from different cultures. Use other Underworld stories.
- Consider how the episode ties in with Virgil's presentation of Roman history.

Further reading

- MacLennan, K. (ed.), *Virgil: Aeneid VI*, Latin Texts (London: Bristol Classical Press, 2003).
- *The Cambridge Companion to Virgil*, ed. Charles Martindale (Cambridge: Cambridge University Press, 1997).
- Hardie, P., *Virgil*, Greece & Rome: New Surveys in the Classics no. 28 (Oxford: Oxford University Press, 1998).
- Translations of the *Aeneid* (widely available).
- Homer, *Odyssey* 11, for another look at the Underworld.

● 3. A hard-working wife—Virgil *Aeneid* 8.407–415

Virgil here gives a different concept of virtue compared with the virtuous portrayed in the Underworld in *Aeneid* 6. We see the idea of virtue from hard work, and here describing a woman.

Themes for exploration

- Women in the ancient world
- Epic similes
- The role of the gods
- Concepts of duty and virtue
- Work in the ancient world

Metre—Hexameters

People and places

Minerva—goddess of wisdom and weaving

Notes on text

The simile is used to describe Vulcan and is appropriate not only for the early rise from bed for Vulcan (*noctem addens operi*: line **5**), but also for the labour he will need to put in to create the armour for Aeneas. The virtuous woman works hard so that her children are appropriately brought up. There is a mild irony in the fact that she keeps the bed of her husband chaste. Vulcan's wife is, of course, Venus, and is not so faithful.

Further teaching suggestions

- See below passage 4 Plautus.

Further reading

- Gould, H. and Whiteley, J. (eds.), *Virgil: Aeneid VIII*, Latin Texts (Bristol: Bristol Classical Press, 1979; reprint of London: Macmillan, 1953 edn).

- Gransden, K. W. (ed.), *Virgil: Aeneid Book VIII*, Cambridge Greek and Latin Classics (Cambridge: Cambridge University Press, 1976).

- *The Cambridge Companion to Virgil*, ed. Charles Martindale (Cambridge: Cambridge University Press,1997).

- Balme, M. C. and James Morwood, *On the Margin*: *Marginalized Groups in Ancient Rome* (Oxford: Oxford University Press, 2003).

- Hardie, P., *Virgil*, Greece & Rome: New Surveys in the Classics no. 28 (Oxford: Oxford University Press, 1998).

- Translations of the *Aeneid* (widely available).

● 4. Different standards for men and women—Plautus *Mercator* 817–829

This picture from comedy perhaps reflects reality as opposed to an idealised world.

Themes for exploration

- The roles of men and women in the ancient world
- Ancient ideas of marriage and divorce
- Ancient ideas of right and wrong behaviour
- Humour in Roman comedy

Metre—Iambic senarii

Notes on text

Although in a very colloquial tone, and reflecting the Latin of a later period, the old woman's words make it clear that women have a tougher life than men do as regards expectations within marriage. Men can take prostitutes for themselves with impunity, whereas even a woman going out of doors can be a cause for divorce. She wishes for the same law—or in effect the same standard—for women as for men. She complains that men are far worse offenders than women. Students should remember that this is part of a comedy—the whole prospect of men being treated in the same way as women is laughable for the audience.

Further reading

- Lowe, N. J., *Comedy*, Greece & Rome: New Surveys in the Classics no. 37 (Cambridge: Cambridge University Press, 2008).

- Segal, Erich, *Roman Laughter: The Comedy of Plautus*, 2nd edn (Oxford: Oxford University Press, 1987).

5. The corruption and cruelty of Verres and Cleomenes—Cicero *In Verrem* 2.5.86–121 (abridged)

This series of extracts provides a wealth of examples of Ciceronian rhetorical technique for students to get to grips with, as well as some vivid character portrayals.

Themes for exploration

- The Roman political system
- Roman attitude to foreigners
- Virtue and 'being Roman'
- The corruption of power
- Cruelty and torture
- Cicero's rhetorical skill and use of language
- The character of Verres
- The lesser characters of Cleomenes and Sextius

People and places

Verres—quaestor in 80 BC, then praetor in 74 BC. Verres won the governorship of Sicily as his pro-praetorian role. He behaved in outrageous fashion extorting all he could out of the people of Sicily. Upon his return to Rome in 70 BC, he was eventually prosecuted by Cicero in August of that year, the latter having gathered much evidence from the province. He was to be defended by Hortensius, but found that he had to flee into exile in Massilia after the first part of the prosecution—this section of the speech was never actually delivered.

Cleomenes—Verres' henchman

Centuripinus—Centuripa was a city/town to the east of Mt Etna in Sicily.

Segestanus—Segesta was a city in western Sicily.

Tyndaritanus—Tyndaris was a town in north western Sicily.

Herbitensis—Herbita was a town to the east of Mt Etna in Sicily.

Heracliensis—Heraclia was a town in southern Sicily.

Apolloniensis—Apollonia was a port in northern Sicily.

Haluntinus—Haluntium was a town in northern Sicily.

Odyssea—a port in south eastern Sicily

Sextius—Verres' bodyguard (lictor) and executioner

Other references are explained in the Students' Book.

Notes on text

Lines 1–24

The list of ships and their origins (*Segestana navis, Tyndaritana ...*: lines **2–3**) in the defence fleet is built up to sound almost grand, only for Cicero to undercut this with a statement about its reality. He makes clear the contrast between how things are in appearance, and how they are in reality (*in speciem sed inops et infirma ...*: lines **3–4**), and the negativity provided by the pair of adjectives beginning *in-* is all to evident. Cicero then embarks upon a sarcastic description of the activities of Verres (*iste praetor diligens ...*: line **5**), making his picture of Verres' banquet most vivid with the superlative *flagitiosissimum* (**6**). Cicero conveys how insultingly Verres behaves towards the sailors of the fleet with the throwaway *paulisper* (**8**). The position of *stetit* (**8**) at the beginning of its sentence allows our focus to come to the shore where Verres is banqueting. It adds an air of grandeur—when we then hear how the praetor is dressed (*soleatus ... cum pallio purpureo tunicaque talari*: **8–9**), we realise how much Cicero is both mocking Verres and exposing his corruption. Along with another reference to Verres with the pejorative *istum* (**9**), we see that this is no unusual occurrence.

Verres' comfort and excess is in marked contrast to the state of the sailors of the fleet. Here Cicero's language highlights their plight—forced to eat palm roots, they are seen as *miseri perditique* (**14**). Cleomenes begins to indulge in the same type of behaviour as Verres, and Cicero emphasises this in various ways—*luxurie ac nequitia/totos dies* (**15/16**). Cicero makes the news of the arrival of the pirates (at Odyssea) appear as shocking as it would have been for Cleomenes and the sailors, with both *ecce* and *repente* (**17**). There is also a marked contrast (**17**) between the state of Cleomenes (*ebrio*) and that of the rest (*esurientibus*). The state in which the land forces have been left by Verres now becomes Cicero's preoccupation—it is all down to the reasoning of that most greedy man (*istius hominis avarissimi ratio*: lines **22–23**).

Passage 25–35

The speed of Verres' actions is suggested by Cicero's use of *repente*, and the position of *procedit* at the beginning of the sentence (line **25**). His enraged state is added to by the tricolon of wickedness (*scelere furore crudelitate*: **25–26**). The short clauses add to the charged atmosphere. The willingness of the sea-captains to help is matched by their innocence and helplessness. Cicero has infinitives (rather than perfects) frame the sentence (*implorare ... rogare*: **28–29**) to make vivid their pleadings. The *clamor et admiratio* (line **30**) of the people is matched by the *impudentiam atque audaciam* (line **31**) of Verres.

Lines 36–48

The position of *includuntur* (line **36**) at the beginning of its sentence puts the focus on the situation of the condemned captains. Their punishment has a twofold effect (*constituitur/ sumitur*: **36/37**) and the latter part is emphasised by the repetition of *prohibentur* (**37**). The desperate plight of their fathers and mothers is then highlighted (lines **38–42**). We then learn part of the reason for their misery (lines **42–44**)—Sextius the lictor, complete with a full list of titles given to him by Cicero (and indeed he is named at the end of the list of such titles). The introduction of direct speech for what Sextius is supposed to have said for his dreadful extortion demands makes the situation particularly graphic (lines **44–45**). When these demands become questions about how the captains might be killed less painfully, or not tortured, Cicero is especially brilliant and realistic, if gruesome (lines **46–48**).

Lines 49–67

Cicero's exclamations about their pain and misfortune are strong and heartfelt (lines **49–50**).

That they are followed by a sentence (**50–51**) remarking upon the fact that the parents are having to purchase not the life of their children but the speed of their death makes them even more so. Sextius manages to work things both ways and sees to it that the young captains ask their parents to provide money to ease their plight (**51–54**). The extent of the anguish caused is stressed by the repetition of *multi* (**54–55**). Cicero even suggests a combination of the reasoning which might go on in the minds of both the captains and Sextius, as regards how further cruelty will get in the way of death, which might have brought an end (**56**). There can even be an obscene suggestion of throwing the bodies to the dogs, and a demand for money for the right to burial (**57–59**).

Cicero's rhetorical questions (**59–63**) emphasise how inhuman Verres is, and how much this situation is one which concerns all men. From the simple statement '*feriuntur securi*' (**63**), the supposed joy which Verres feels is exposed and emphasised, especially with verbs in the second person singular. The repetition of *errabas* (**65**) reveals Cicero's confidence in everything he is saying—Verres is guilty, and there is no getting away from it.

Further teaching suggestions
- Collect Latin examples of Cicero's language demonstrating exaggeration.
- Ask pupils to research the role of Sicily in the ancient world, particularly in Roman times.
- Construct a possible defence speech for Verres or Cleomenes and/or reasons to explain their actions.

Further reading
- Levens, R. (ed.), *Cicero: The Fifth Verrine Oration*, Latin Texts (London: Bristol Classical Press, 1992; reprint of London: Methuen, 1946 edn).
- Translations of Cicero's speeches (widely available).
- Steel, C., *Roman Oratory*, Greece and Rome: New Surveys in the Classics no. 36 (Cambridge: Cambridge University Press, 2006).
- Harris, Robert, *Imperium* (London: Hutchinson, 2006).

6. The bravery of Mucius Scaevola and Cloelia—Livy *A History of Rome* 2.12–13 (abridged)

The two characters with whom students are presented in these passages are brave and selfless. The stories are accessible and have a vivid narrative.

Themes for exploration
- Virtue and bravery
- The similarities and differences found in the bravery of the men and women of these extracts
- The early history of Rome
- The reasons for such stories appearing in a history of Rome
- What being a Roman citizen means in this context
- Livy's use of direct speech and his vivid narrative
- The characters of Mucius and Cloelia

People and places

Tiber—the river Tiber

Porsenna—king of the Etruscans—in particular of Clusium, *c.* 500 BC

Coclites—Horatius Cocles was a myth-historical defender of Rome of the period, who fought alone on a bridge against the enemy.

Via Sacra—the main street of Rome

Notes on text

Lines 1–21

Livy presents Mucius as a bold individual as he informs the senators what he intends to do. The two infinitives *transire Tiberim … et intrare* (line **1**) are balanced by two nouns preceded by negatives revealing what he does not plan (*non praedo nec populationum … ultor*: **2–3**). Mucius makes it clear that a greater deed is his plan (line **3**). The brevity of the Senate's approval (**3–4**) and the use of the present tense ensure that the narrative moves quickly. The hidden sword (**4**) and the very dense crowd (**5**) add to the intensity of events, whilst the possibility of mistaken identity allows Livy to increase his bravery in our eyes. The verb *obtruncat* (**10**) is graphic indeed. The image is one of a rather cool customer as he clears a pathway by the mere existence of his bloody blade (lines **10–11**). Livy's alliterative phrasing after he has been dragged back before the king emphasises his bravery— *metuendus magis quam metuens* (**13–14**). His bold statement, *Romanus sum civis* (**14**), is effective for its simplicity, and the tale which Livy tells becomes a very Roman one as he has Mucius say that it is Roman to do and suffer brave things (*et facere et pati fortia Romanum est*: **16**). He reinforces that he is not alone in his intention, and threatens with an effective hendiadys (*ferrum hostemque*: **19**) that the enemy will soon be upon Porsenna. Mucius points out that it is Porsenna that they are after, and repeatedly stresses this (**20–21**).

Lines 22–35

When the angered king has fires prepared (**22–23**), Mucius' words match his actions and he thrusts his hand into the fire (**23–25**). The king's shocked reaction (**25–26**) is accompanied by words of respect sending Mucius on his way (**26–30**). Mucius warns Porsenna, almost as a matter of kindness (**30–31**), that the Romans will not give up. His direct speech (**31–35**) enlivens the narrative and further emphasises his selflessness.

Lines 36–52

Cloelia is seen to be spurred on by the bravery of Mucius (**36–37**), and after evading the enemy guards, and swimming across the Tiber, leads other women back to their kinsfolk (**38–40**). At first Cloelia is demanded as a sole hostage amidst the king's initial anger (**40–42**), but then we find that her deed is admired above those of Horatius Cocles and Gaius Mucius (**43**).

The final focus (**46–52**) is very much on Cloelia and the fact that she, as a woman, has brought about peace, is highlighted by repetition *novam/ novo* (**50**). Cloelia's memorial too is suitably distinctive (**50–52**).

Further teaching suggestions

- Consider the stories of Mucius and Cloelia and ask students to construct a summary list or PowerPoint presentation of brave speech and brave action for each.

- Have students compile a newspaper front page on either story which reveals that they have understood exactly what happened in each tale.

Further reading

- Whiteley, J. L. (ed.), *Livy: Book II*, Latin Texts (London: Bristol Classical Press, 1995; reprint of London: Macmillan, 1963 edn).

- Luce, T. J. (trans.), *Livy: The Rise of Rome: Books One to Five*, Oxford World's Classics (Oxford: Oxford University Press, 1998).

- Kraus, C. S. and Woodman, A. J., *Latin Historians*, Greece & Rome: New Surveys in the Classics no. 27 (Oxford: Oxford University Press, 1997).

2 FAMILY LIFE AND RELATIONSHIPS

Contents overview

🔊 Verse

1. Grief at parting: Ovid *Tristia*
2. Love and loss: Catullus
3. Sulpicia discovers love: Sulpicia
4. Love for a young man: Horace *Odes*

Prose

5. A close-knit family: Pliny *Letters*
6. An ideal daughter: Pliny *Letters*
7. Education within the family: Tacitus *Dialogus*
8. Bitter hatred: Cicero *Pro Milone*

Themes in this section

Relationships with a lover	2, 3, 4
Relationships with a husband or wife	1, 5
General family relationships and the Roman family	1, 2, 5, 6, 7
Sorrow, sadness and separation	1, 2, 5, 6
Strong female characters	3, 4, 5, 6, 7
Hatred and jealousy	2, 4, 8
Love	2, 3, 4, 5, 6

🔊 1. Grief at parting—Ovid *Tristia* 1.3.1–84 (abridged)

Ovid was supposedly sent into exile by Augustus for *carmen et error* (thought to be a reference to the *Ars Amatoria*, and some connection with a scandal involving Augustus' granddaughter, Julia), and in the *Tristia*, he writes how awful life is in his place of exile (Tomis on the Black Sea). There are those who pose the scenario that Ovid's writings from exile do not speak of a historical event but rather consist of a literary exercise in exile poetry. Students should be aware of the possibility but should not be overly worried by it.

Themes for exploration

- Exile poetry
- Parting from loved ones and associated emotions
- Ovid's sadness and whether his emotion is genuine
- The relationship between Ovid and his wife

- Self-reference and the actual physicality of the situation
- Those things which are missed when going away from home
- The Roman family centred around its household gods

Metre—Elegiacs

People and places

Caesar—Augustus Caesar

Ausonia—Italy

Luna—the Roman moon goddess

Quirinus—an early god of the citadel of Rome who came to be identified with Romulus, the founder of Rome

Mettus—dictator of Alba, who broke his treaty with King Tullus of Rome, trying to support both Rome and Rome's enemies, the people of Fidenae

Other references are explained in the Students' Book.

Notes on text

Lines 1–34

Here Ovid recalls, with tears, the night on which he had to leave Rome (**1–4**)—and go beyond the bounds of Ausonia, as commanded by Augustus (**5–6**). He feels mentally unprepared and physically his heart is not ready for the move—a situation highlighted by the repetition of *nec*, the pair of gerunds (*parandi* and *legendi*) and the choice of *torpuerant* (**7–9**). The anaphora of *non* emphasises his lack of preparation—he is without the people and things he needs, yet also without those things of which he will be partly deprived in his existence in exile (**10–11**).

As Ovid steels himself for the moment of his departure, the juxtaposition of *flentem flens* (**17**) helps the picture of his (third) wife's misery to develop. The almost meteorological references (*nubem*, *imbre*: **13, 18**) prepare us for Ovid looking at the buildings of Rome against the night sky later in the passage. It is particularly upsetting that Ovid's daughter is away at the time in Libya (**19–20**). The sibilance and assonance of *luctus gemitusque* (**21**) are effective in the build-up to the knowledge that every corner of the house is filled with the sound of crying (**24**). The juxtaposition of *parvis* and *grandibus* (**25**) is striking, as is the comparison with the capture of Troy (**26**), especially as Ovid is about to move to a view of the Capitol (the Capitoline hill and its buildings) under moonlight (we almost might say 'by its light' for *ad hanc*) (**28–29**). The Capitol, we are told, was near to Ovid's house, which he refers to by describing it as his household god(s)—*nostro ... Lari* (**30**). Ovid will miss the city of Rome and its buildings. He addresses them and bids farewell for all time to the city of Quirinus (an ancient Sabine deity largely associated with Romulus) (**30–34**).

Lines 35–59

The second passage allows us to see something of a contrast between Ovid and his wife. Note the emphatic positions of *ego* and *uxor*, and the difference between *hac prece* and *pluribus* (**35**). The word order of the ablative absolute (*singultu impediente*) interrupts *medios sonos* (**36**). Some may remark here upon the sibilance reflecting something of his wife's distress. The focus on Ovid's wife is stressed by the position of *illa* (**37**). Not only is her hair distressed, but she also defiles herself with the ashes from the hearth (**38**). Students should be aware of the repeated focus on

the Lares and the Penates (i.e. the household gods which Ovid is leaving), and that all her efforts are to no avail (highlighted by *adversos*, *effudit*, and *non valitura*: **39–40**).

Ovid's farewells are made dramatic by the repetition of *ter*, *saepe* and *dedi*, as well as by alliteration (**42–46**). The verbs in the first person add to the effect.

The comparison with Mettus is a vivid one (**50–51**). Livy (1.27 ff.) tells the tale of how Mettus, dictator of Alba, was pulled apart bodily by two chariots, each drawn by four horses, after treachery against Tullus, king of Rome. He had promised to support the Romans, but instead supported their enemy, the people of Fidenae.

The repetition of *tum vero* (**52, 54**) switches the focus from Ovid's pain to that of his grieving wife. Her words too are emphatic with the anaphora of *simul*, and her wish to be with Ovid wherever he is (**56–59**). She reveals therein some ideas about marriage similar to those found in Arria later in this section (passage 5, A close-knit family).

> ### Further teaching suggestions
> - Ovid is looking back to the time when he left Rome. Have students construct a mock Facebook page/blog describing the events which happened to aid their revision.
> - Discuss how serious/light-hearted Ovid is throughout the extract.

> ### Further reading
> - Virgil, *Aeneid* 2—farewell between Aeneas and Creusa.
> - Virgil, *Georgics* 4 and Ovid *Metamorphoses* 10—parting of Orpheus and Eurydice.
> - Ovid, *Metamorphoses* 11—the parting of Ceyx and Alcyone.
> - Williams, Gareth D., *Banished Voices: Readings in Ovid's Exile Poetry*, Cambridge Classical Studies (Cambridge: Cambridge University Press, 1994).
> - Claassen, Jo-Marie, *Ovid Revisited; The Poet in Exile* (London: Duckworth, 2008).

2. Love and loss

a. Farewell to a brother—Catullus 101 ad inferias

The formulaic nature of this address made at the graveside of his brother allows us to see a most tender and emotional Catullus. His brother had died in the Troad, the area near Troy.

Themes for exploration

- Grief and the intensity of Catullus' language
- Family relationships
- Religious belief and death in the ancient world

Metre—Elegiacs

Notes on text

Lines 1–10

Amidst his grief the repetition in *multas per/multa per* (**1**) lets him keep control as he performs the obligatory funerary offering to the shade of his brother, having not been present at the funeral itself. This is a good poem upon which students may cut their teeth in terms of their skills of literary criticism. The plentiful *m* alliteration in lines **3** and **9** has a genuine effect here as do the time phrases at the beginning of line **7**: it is as if Catullus is searching for the words appropriate for such a difficult situation. We may also point to the broken nature of line **2** and the imagery of *mutam cinerem* in line **4**, whilst the personal pronouns (especially the intensified *tete*) in line **5** add to the emotion. The formulaic poignancy of the last line is striking for its final words, but throughout that formulaic element of duty and words said at a graveside are noticeable.

Further teaching suggestions

- Have students reconstruct what they can of Catullus' life from these poems, and in particular have them discuss when they think these poems are written in relation to each other.
- From Catullus 101, discuss which aspects of this poem are a formal graveside 'prayer'.
- Using the audio CD (tracks 11–14), how does the sound of Catullus' poetry reflect the sense?

Further reading

- Quinn, Kenneth (ed.), *Catullus, The Poems*, rev edn (London: Bristol Classical Press, 1996).
- Translations of the poems of Catullus (widely available).
- Balme, M. G. and Morwood, James, *Oxford Latin Reader* (Oxford: Oxford University Press, 1997).
- Wiseman, T. P., *Catullus and His World* (Cambridge: Cambridge University Press, 1987).
- Hurley, Amanda Kolson, *Catullus* (London: Bristol Classical Press, 2004).

b. Rejection in love—Catullus 8 ad se ipsum

Here Catullus struggles in his own mind with the concept of the end of his affair with Lesbia. There is some light-heartedness and self-mockery.

Metre—Limping iambics (choliambics/scazons)

Notes on text

Lines 1–19

The direct address to himself is immediately followed by two instructions in the subjunctive (*desinas, ducas*: **1–2**), while the close sequence of *periisse perditum* (**2**) adds an air of finality. While line **3** might be seen as wishful thinking, the idea is that the affair is over now, and the repetition in line **8** brings this home. The frequentative *ventitabas* (**4**) is worth noting—Catullus used to hang on her every movement, and she provided the happy times, although the second part of line **7** perhaps hints that the love was all flowing in one direction. In line **9**, *iam* intensifies *nunc* and the string of prohibitions is followed by even more forceful positive imperatives. The farewell of line **12** is believable, and Catullus' use of the third person reinforces this, especially when the verb is the same as the imperative of the previous line. However if this is done to reassure Catullus himself, then there may be some lingering doubts, and t he same holds for his language in line **13**. His questions in the latter part of the poem are directed at Lesbia, but he knows he will not receive answers—they are part of the play of convincing himself. The final line of the poem once again addresses Catullus.

Further reading

- Quinn, Kenneth (ed.), *Catullus, The Poems*, rev edn (London: Bristol Classical Press, 1996).
- Translations of the poems of Catullus (widely available).
- Balme, M. G. and Morwood, James, *Oxford Latin Reader* (Oxford: Oxford University Press, 1997).
- Wiseman, T. P., *Catullus and His World* (Cambridge: Cambridge University Press, 1987).
- Hurley, Amanda Kolson, *Catullus* (London: Bristol Classical Press, 2004).

c. Jealousy takes over—Catullus 51 ad Lesbiam

This is the poem which gives Lesbia her name. It is a translation of a poem by Sappho, and Catullus reflects her Greek accurately enough, whilst at the same time making the poem his own. It is possibly his first poem to Lesbia.

Themes for exploration

- Catullus' jealous feelings, both physical and emotional
- How close to Sappho's original is Catullus' reworking?

Metre—Sapphics

Notes on text

Lines 1–16

The repetition of *ille* allows the opening focus of the poem to be on the situation in which Catullus would like to find himself. He cannot bear the fact that any other man watches and listens to Lesbia The second stanza brings out the raw emotion with *eripit* (**6**), and we have employed the conjecture *vocis in ore* (**8**) so as to present a complete text to the student, although Quinn prefers *Lesbia vocis*.

The physical signs are very much to the fore in stanza 3, where vivid flame imagery (**10**), sibilance (*sonitu suopte*) and onomatopoeia make Catullus' feelings vivid. Some wonder whether stanza 4 belongs to the poem as it is not part of the translation of the Sappho piece. For further discussion, see Quinn. Catullus speaks of how leisure brings him trouble as it does others—he is idling away looking at Lesbia, and it causes such physical symptoms.

Further teaching suggestions

- Have students reconstruct what they can of Catullus' life from these poems, and in particular have them discuss when they think these poems are written in relation to each other.
- Using the audio CD (tracks 11–14), how does the sound of Catullus' poetry reflect the sense?

Further reading

- Quinn, Kenneth (ed.), *Catullus, The Poems*, rev edn (London: Bristol Classical Press, 1996).
- Translations of the poems of Catullus (widely available).
- Balme, M. G. and Morwood, James, *Oxford Latin Reader* (Oxford: Oxford University Press, 1997).
- Wiseman, T. P., *Catullus and His World* (Cambridge: Cambridge University Press, 1987).
- Hurley, Amanda Kolson, *Catullus* (London: Bristol Classical Press, 2004).

d. Ever-changing love—Catullus 70 and 85

Both poems will allow students to derive a great deal from a small amount of text, and yet at the same time feel they have discussed weighty matters. These poems provide an excellent starting point for any student embarking upon a study of Latin literature at GCSE level.

Themes for exploration

- Love
- Hatred
- Expectations in a relationship

Metre—Elegiacs

People and places

Iuppiter—Jupiter, king of the gods

Notes on text

Poem 70 lines 1–4

The poet comments on his own situation in a very simple way. His relationship is full of protestations of faithfulness. However the repetition of *dicit* in lines **1** and **3**, followed by a pause in the second instance, allows us to hear Catullus' doubts. *dicit* occurs again in line **3**, as part of an almost proverbial expression.

Poem 85 lines 1–2

These lines are famous and show the contradictions at the heart of Catullus' relationship. He asks himself the question but cannot give a reply, as love is so tormenting.

Further teaching suggestions

- Have students reconstruct what they can of Catullus' life from these poems, and in particular have them discuss when they think these poems are written in relation to each other.

- 🔊 Using the audio CD (tracks 11–14), how does the sound of Catullus' poetry reflect the sense?

Further reading

- Quinn, Kenneth (ed.), *Catullus, The Poems*, rev edn (London: Bristol Classical Press, 1996).
- Translations of the poems of Catullus (widely available).
- Balme, M. G. and Morwood, James, *Oxford Latin Reader* (Oxford: Oxford University Press, 1997).
- Wiseman, T. P., *Catullus and His World* (Cambridge: Cambridge University Press, 1987).
- Hurley, Amanda Kolson, *Catullus* (London: Bristol Classical Press, 2004).

3. Sulpicia discovers love—Sulpicia 1

Reading Sulpicia will prove a first for many, and we hope a rewarding one. In this poem she reveals a passion with all the freshness of new love.

Themes for exploration

- First love
- Gossip
- Women in love
- Women in ancient Rome
- Women's writing

Metre—Elegiacs

People and places

Cytherea—Cythera is an island to the south of the Peloponnese in Greece. It was thought to be an island of Venus, and so she is referred to here as Cytherean.

Camenae—originally rustic goddesses of springs and fountains, the Camenae become identified with the Muses, and this is how they are referred to here.

Venus—goddess of love

Notes on text

Lines 1–10

The opening is simple enough, and we see that love has come at last. Fearing shame lest she hide her love, it is better, she feels, that she reveal it to the world. In lines **3–4**, we see that Venus has dropped love in her lap—possibly after other poetic efforts (and so the due mention of the Muses). Sulpicia has more than enough love for Venus to reveal should others have missed out. She does not want to entrust anything to writing tablets lest someone else read them before her lover (**7–8**). She is very conscious of how she must appear to others (**9–10**).

Readers should note that the text here follows that of the Oxford Classical Text, where in line 8 we find *ne legat ut nemo ...* . Some other texts do read *id* for *ut* here. In either case, the sense is the same, namely that Sulpicia does not want to entrust the news of her love to writing lest someone else should read it before her lover *meus*. Specifically with the reading *ut* we might say 'lest he read it as/ like no one (should) before my lover'.

Further teaching suggestions

- That this poem is one of the few surviving written by a woman from the ancient world presents us with a wealth of areas for discussion, including remarks on what we can learn about the life of and expectations of women in ancient Rome.

- Have students construct a summary of this poem in the form of a Facebook announcement.

Further reading

- Stevenson, Jane, *Women Latin Poets: Language, Gender and Authority from Antiquity to the Eighteenth Century* (Oxford: Oxford University Press, 2008).

- Skoie, Mathilde, *Reading Sulpicia: Commentaries 1475–1990* (Oxford: Oxford University Press, 2002).

⬤ 4. Love for a young man—Horace *Odes* 1.8

This poem is from the first book of Horace's *Odes* and presents students with the conundrum of whom Horace is more interested in—the boy, Sybaris, or the girl to whom he addresses the ode.

Themes for exploration

- Love and jealousy
- 'Manly' activities
- Who is Horace more interested in, Lydia or Sybaris?

Metre—Sapphics (maior) (i.e. Aristophanics alternating with Greater Sapphics)

People and places

Lydia—the girl to whom Horace addresses the poem

Sybaris—the boy in Lydia's clutches

Gallicus—Gallic

Tiber—the river Tiber flowing through Rome

filium Thetidis—the son of the sea-nymph, Thetis, i.e. Achilles, who supposedly went into hiding in women's clothing before the Trojan War

Lycius—Lycian. Lycia was an area of south western Turkey in what was Asia Minor. The Lycians were allies of the Trojans.

Other references are explained in the Students' Book.

Notes on text

Lines 1–16

Horace feels Sybaris should be indulging in manly, military activities, and not giving his time to love. This is rather the dilemma which Hippolytus faces, except seen from the other side. The latter gives too much of his time to hunting (and worship of Diana/Artemis) whilst ignoring the activities of love, in which a young man should be involved (and

the worship of Venus/Aphrodite). Lydia is seen to be ruining Sybaris with love when he should taking part in military exercises on the Campus Martius (**3–4**), and riding as a military young man amongst his peers (**5–6**). Horace's direct tone is revealed with *dic* (line **1**), and by his questions, repeatedly beginning with *cur* (**2, 3, 5** and **8**). The *p* alliteration in line **4** may reflect the tough knocks of exercise, whilst the *t* alliteration of line **8** may reflect the fear which Sybaris is now displaying. He should be wrestling, receiving bruises, and participating in other athletic exercise.

Further teaching suggestions

- Discuss whether Horace is more interested in Lydia than Sybaris.
- Compare and contrast the portrayal of women in love presented both by this poem and that of Sulpicia (2.3).
- Consider the poem in the light of the Hippolytus myth: Hippolytus was destroyed by Aphrodite/Venus for not paying her due attention. Young men in love, it is suggested, should pay attention to both the goddess of love, and the goddess of hunting (Artemis/Diana).

Further reading

- West, David (trans.), *Horace: The Complete Odes and Epodes*, Oxford World's Classics (Oxford: Oxford University Press, 2008).
- Hills, Philip D., *Horace*, Ancients in Action (Bristol: Bristol Classical Press, 2005).
- Lyne, R. O. A. M., *Latin Love Poets from Catullus to Horace* (Oxford: Clarendon Press, 1980).

5. A close-knit family—Pliny *Letters* 3.16

Arria's firmly-held beliefs about marriage come to the fore even more in the second part of this extract. Students will be able to find a very strong character within these passages.

Themes for exploration

- Family relationships, especially husband/wife
- The role of wife and mother in the Roman world
- The characters of Caecina Paetus and Arria
- Attitudes to death
- Endurance in the face of suffering
- Pliny's narrative technique and how he enlivens his story

People and places

Caecina Paetus—the husband in this story

Scribonianus—Lucius Arruntius Camillus Scribonianus, consul in AD 32, and later governor of Dalmatia, led a revolt against Claudius in AD 42.

Illyricum—Roman province on the east coast of the Adriatic Sea

Claudius—emperor AD 41–54

Arria—the wife in this story; Pliny finds out all his information from her grand-daughter Fannia

Thrasea—her son-in-law, Publius Clodius Thrasea Paetus, a senator and philosopher

Notes on text

Lines 1–17

The close family relationship is evident from the second sentence and the strength of Arria is also apparent from her leadership of the funeral (*huic illa funus paravit, …*: **4**), and her subsequent protection of her husband from the reality of what has happened to their son (**4–8**). Pliny makes the tale interesting by reporting her actual words to her husband (**7–8**). He is also careful to show that she is not simply hard, but rather that when her tears do begin to break through, she removes herself from the room and gives herself to grief (**8–9**). Her bravery is clear too from Pliny's next example of her deeds—but he finds more to praise in this present conduct with regard to hiding her grief, because there is no immortal glory attached to the deed (**15–17**).

Lines 18–38

Pliny tells how Caecina Paetus had been involved in Scribonianus' revolt (**18–19**). Arria's desire to follow her husband (**20**) once more shows the closeness of their relationship. The account is enlivened not only by her words (**21–23**) but by the fact that, when she does not succeed, she immediately hires a small fishing vessel (**23–24**). Her direct speech to the wife of Scribonianus reveals her concept of marital duty—why is Scribonianus' wife still alive when Scribonianus is dead? (*ego … te audiam … et vivis?*: **26–27**). The report of the tale of Thrasea's question and her answer shows that her ideas of marriage were deep-rooted and in her opinion should apply to everyone (**30–32**). Her various remarks to her family when she is under guard from them and when she has tried to kill herself reveal her convictions (**33–37**). Pliny asks the question whether these deeds are greater than that status she achieved from her 'Paetus, it doesn't hurt' actions.

6. An ideal daughter—Pliny *Letters* 5.16

There is much to get out of this letter, whether it be the close relationship between father and daughter or the praise which Pliny lavishes on the latter's strength of character. Pliny's language is accessible and has a style which may enable students to see readily various techniques at work.

Themes for exploration

- Family relationships, especially father/daughter

- The characters of Fundanus and his daughter

- Death and memorials to life

- Endurance in the face of suffering

- Pliny's descriptive technique

People and places

Gaius Plinius—the author and letter writer (See the Appendix on The Latin Writers in the Students' Book, pp. 154–155.)

Aefulanus Marcellinus—the friend to whom he writes

Fundanus—the friend whose daughter has died

Notes on text

Lines 1–26

Pliny's immediate use of the superlative (*tristissimus*, line **1**) sets the tone for his depth of feeling in his words about Fundanus' younger daughter. He begins his praises with three comparatives (*festivius, amabilius* and *dignius*: **3–4**) before moving on to a brief statement about her age (**4**)—making it all the more remarkable—and a tricolon of adjectives showing how the daughter had such supreme womanly qualities spanning three generations (*anilis, matronalis, puellaris*: **5–6**). The addition of alliteration in *virginali verecundia* (**6**) is suitably noble and reverential. The repeated exclamations of how appropriately affectionate she was to various parties (*ut illa patris...!* etc.: **6–9**) emphasise the esteem in which she was held by others as well as Pliny, and thus justify his eulogy. For variety he later moves to exclamations using *quam* (**9–10**), followed by continued praise for various aspects of her behaviour using abstract nouns (*temperantia, patientia, constantia*: **11–12**). Pliny even makes elegant his description of how she reacts to her illness with a chiasmus (*corporis viribus vigore animi*: **13**).

Pliny's later exclamations about her funeral are marked by a tricolon of adjectives (*triste plane acerbumque*: **16–17**), whilst his repetition of *iam* (**17–18**) emphasises that the day of her funeral was to have been that of her wedding (**18**). The three things on which Fundanus was to have spent money (*vestes, margarita, gemmas*: **22**) are now in marked contrast with what he has to spend the money on (*tus et unguenta et odores*: **22–23**). There is a considerable shift in Fundanus himself too (**23–26**).

Further teaching suggestions

- Collect Latin examples from Pliny's description of the virtues of Fundanus' daughter.
- Compare and contrast Fundanus' daughter and Arria (passage 5).
- What do we learn of Fundanus from this letter?

Further reading

- Sherwin-White, A. N. (ed.), *The Letters of Pliny: A Social and Historical Commentary* (Oxford: Oxford University Press, 1966). A large and thorough work, with articles on key aspects of Pliny's letters, which has informed subsequent studies but is useful to consult on points of detail.
- Radice, B. (trans.), *The Letters of the Younger Pliny*, Penguin Classics, rev. repr. (Harmondsworth: Penguin, 1969).

7. Education within the family—Tacitus *Dialogus* 28

This passage forms part of one of Tacitus' shorter works, the *Dialogus de oratoribus*, which is a treatise on oratory. Here he further explores one of his main ideas, namely that the art of oratory has become decadent as a result of the decline of education within the family.

Themes for exploration

- The role of the mother within the family
- Roman education
- The development of moral values

People and places

Gracchi—primarily referring to Tiberius Sempronius Gracchus, and Gaius Gracchus, the reforming politicians of the second century BC, who were both killed after attempting (and succeeding in some) radical legislation

Cornelia—mother of the Gracchi, second daughter of Scipio Africanus

Caesar—Julius Caesar, the famous Roman politician and general (See the Appendix on The Latin Writers in the Students' Book, pp. 154–155.)

Aurelia—Aurelia Cotta, mother of Julius Caesar

Augustus—first emperor of Rome

Atia—Atia Balba Caesonia, niece of Julius Caesar and mother of Augustus

Notes on text

Lines 1–25

Tacitus begins this passage by asking the question who could be ignorant of the decline in oratory, whilst at the same time posing four causes (the laziness of youth, the negligence of parents, the lack of knowledge of teachers, and forgetfulness of old customs: **2–4**). Such poor habits have permeated (*manant*: **5**) to the provinces. Tacitus sets about telling us a few things about the strictness and discipline that the ancestors put into the rearing of children (**5–9**).

The contrast between the use of a bought wet-nurse and the role of a child mother in the early stage of education is made clear (*non in cella emptae nutricis sed gremio ac sinu matris*: **11**). A mother was seen as having a twofold duty—towards home and children. An older female relative of high esteem and character (*probatis spectatisque moribus*: **13–14**) would be found. Tacitus again stresses that such women would look after all aspects (*non ... modo ... sed ... etiam ...*: **16–18**) of a child's education. A trio of mothers who reared leaders of high renown are set forth as examples (**18–20**). Tacitus harks back to *disciplina ac severitas* (**20–21**) as being what produces a pure, virtuous nature, affected by no depravity, equipping young men for a wholesome professional life, whether a life of soldiering, law or rhetoric (**21–24**).

> ### Further teaching suggestions
>
> - Compare and contrast what things children learn at home today with what Tacitus suggests was inculcated in the traditional ancient Roman home.
> - Discuss whether Tacitus is simply harking back to a golden age.
> - Have students research the famous individuals and their mothers who are mentioned in the passage, and present their findings in a PowerPoint presentation.

> ### Further reading
>
> - Mayer, R. (ed.), *Tacitus, Dialogus de oratoribus* (Cambridge: Cambridge University Press, 2001).
> - Ash, Rhiannon, *Tacitus*, Ancients in Action (London: Bristol Classical Press, 2006).
> - Martin, Ronald, *Tacitus* (London: Bristol University Press, 1994, a reprint with corrections of London: Batsford, 1981).
> - Kraus, C. S. and Woodman, A. J. *Latin Historians*, Greece and Rome New Surveys no. 27 (Oxford: Oxford University Press, 1997).

8. Bitter hatred—Cicero *Pro Milone* 34–35

This passage is from Cicero's speech, *Pro Milone*, which the orator wrote in defence of Titus Annius Milo who was held responsible for the death of Publius Clodius Pulcher in January 52 BC following a violent fracas between the two and their supporters on the Appian Way.

Themes for exploration

- Political hatred/alliance, and the reasons for that
- Cicero's language and rhetorical style
- The characters of Cicero and Milo

People and places

Clodius—Publius Clodius Pulcher, notorious politician and demagogue. He had been tribune in 58 BC, and was standing for the praetorship of 52BC, and Milo for the consulship. The two were bitter enemies and responsible for gang-warfare which beset Rome in the 50s BC.

Milo—Titus Annius Milo, tribune 57 BC, aedile 56 BC, praetor 54 BC. Defended by Cicero here.

lex Plotia—the *lex Plotia de vi* was the law under which Milo had attempted to prosecute Clodius for attacking his house at the end of 57 BC. The case had not been brought to trial because Clodius had been aedile, and because, as Colson remarks, there was probably little case against him.

Notes on text

Lines 1–23

Cicero here focuses on the question why it might have been in Milo's interest that Clodius be killed so that he can rebut any such suggestion as ridiculous. He follows his two questions with the charge that others make against Milo—namely that Clodius stood in the way of his winning the consulship. Cicero turns their argument on its head: it was because Milo had somebody (Clodius) to fight against that he was winning. He then reminds the jury of Milo's services to both Cicero and the state (as if the two are one and the same!) (*erga me remque publicam meritorum memoria*: **7**). He also reminds the jury, with a rhetorical question, of all the dangers posed by the possible praetorship of Clodius, using particularly strong language, i.e. very great fear of revolution (*maximo rerum novarum metu*: **11**). Milo, Cicero suggests, was the only hope for the people of Rome (**13–14**). He even goes on to remark that with Clodius removed from the scene, (*Clodio remoto*: **15**), things are more of a struggle for Milo: his glory was increasing by stopping Clodius' excesses (**17–18**). The jury may have gained a fear-free existence, but Milo has lost his source of glory (**18–20**)!

Lines 24–34

Cicero puts forward the charge that is being levelled at Milo—i.e. that he killed Clodius because there was strong hatred on his part and because he wanted vengeance (*at valuit odium* ...: **24–25**). Rather, he argues, the boot was most definitely on the other foot in this regard (**25–26**). Although in reality Clodius and Milo were probably as bad as each other, Cicero, as Milo's defence counsel, argues that Milo had no reason to hate Clodius (other than the normal civic hatred one might naturally feel against a wicked man) (**27–29**), but rather that he wanted him alive, because it was in defeating Clodius that Milo found reason to be elected and achieve glory. Clodius on the other hand, Cicero argues, hated Milo, because the latter physically defended Cicero (*defensorem salutis meae*: **29–30**), because he worked against Clodius' madness (*vexatorem furoris*: **30**), and because Milo was prosecuting him under the *lex Plotia* (**31–32**). Cicero's venom against Clodius is clear from his use of *tyrannum illum* (**32**).

> ### Further teaching suggestions
> - Have students research, using a translation of the speech, what actually happened on the Appian Way, between Clodius and Milo.
> - Discuss to what extent Cicero's arguments in this extract are valid and/or logical.

> ### Further reading
> - Colson, F. H. (ed.), *Cicero: Pro Milone*, Latin Texts (London: Duckworth, 1991).
> - Translations of Cicero's speeches (widely available).
> - Steel, C., *Roman Oratory*, Greece and Rome: New Surveys in the Classics no. 36, (Cambridge: Cambridge University Press, 2006).

3 PASSIONS AND POISONS

Content overview

Prose

1. The poisoning of Claudius: Tacitus *Annals*
2. The passion behind a trumped up charge of poison: Cicero *Pro Cluentio*

🔊 **Verse**

3. A snake's poison stirs passion: Virgil *Aeneid*
4. Medea's impassioned plea to Jason: Ovid *Heroides*
5. Catullus struggles with love: Catullus

6. Passion fades: Catullus
7. The passions of a ghostly fury: Ovid *Ibis*

Themes in this section

Poisoning	1, 2, 3, 4
Excessive passion	2, 3, 4, 5, 6, 7
Marital issues	1, 2, 4
The threat of violence	1, 2, 3
Impassioned female characters	2, 3, 4

1. The poisoning of Claudius—Tacitus *Annals* 12.64–69 (abridged)

The problems of the imperial household and the intrigue surrounding the death of Claudius in AD 54 are masterfully presented by Tacitus amidst portents and gossip. The story which he tells is gripping and full of characters who are developed at times by a mere word, and at times by extended description.

Themes for exploration

- Tacitus' sequence of events, and use of detail
- His style and brevity
- His use of a cast of characters who are very much celebrity names
- His eye for dramatic development
- The idea of the *noverca*

- Claudius' problems with his wives
- Claudius' dependence of freedmen
- The motivation of various individuals within the story and comparison with those with power and influence in modern society
- The way in which Tacitus distances himself from the narrative at various points.

People and places

Claudius—emperor AD 41–54, Tiberius Claudius Drusus Caesar, son of Drusus, and younger brother of Germanicus; stepfather to Nero, and father of Britannicus

Agrippina—Agrippina the Younger, Claudius' niece and his fourth wife, mother of Nero, married Claudius in AD 49; previously married to Gnaeus Domitius Ahenobarbus

Pallas—Agrippina's lover: a freedman, and Claudius' secretary for finance

Nero—emperor AD 54–68, son of Agrippina and Gnaeus Domitius Ahenobarbus

Narcissus—a very influential freedman in the service of Claudius (secretary for correspondence) who was responsible for informing on Messalina; committed suicide soon after Claudius' death

Messalina—Claudius' third wife (from AD 41–48), killed after an affair and bigamous marriage with Silius, having been accused of conspiring against Claudius; mother of Britannicus and Octavia

Silius—Gaius Silius, consul designate AD 48, lover of Messalina, also accused of conspiring against Claudius

Lepida—Domitia Lepida, mother of Messalina

Britannicus—son of Claudius and Messalina

Octavia—daughter of Claudius and Messalina

Antonia—daughter of Claudius and his second wife, Aelia Paetina

Marcus Asinius Marcellus—consul for AD 54

Manius Acilius Aviola—consul for AD 54

Locusta—an infamous poisoner

Halotus—taster and chief steward in the imperial household, retained under Nero

Xenophon—a doctor in the imperial household in the service of Agrippina

Sinuessa—on the coast between Rome and Naples

Notes on text

Lines 1–10

Tacitus briefly indicates the date, registering the consular year with an ablative absolute (line **1**). The feeling that 'things ain't what they used to be' (line **1**) is set against the vivid backdrop of an increasingly bizarre (and thus suitably appropriate) list of portents (lines **2–5**). Such lists of portents, together with the consular dating, are a typical feature of Roman annalistic history: their effect here is obvious. His masterful (and journalistic) juxtaposition of events sets the scene for the drama which will unfold (almost, as Ronald Mellor suggests, like a Greek tragedy). With such a list of omens, followed by a list of dying magistrates (lines **5–7**), it seems only fitting that the next occurrence is the death of an emperor. Tacitus moves from the general to the personal and focuses on Agrippina. Her fear as a result of Claudius' drunken threats is highlighted by alliteration and a neat juxtaposition (*praecipuo pavore Agrippina*: lines **7–8**), whilst the plural *coniugum* (line **9**) is suitably vague to help create an atmosphere of suspicion and machination. That *metuens* (line **9**) comes after Claudius' grumble and subsequent threat (*ferret ... puniret*: line **9**) allows the reader to witness the actual sequence of events. The pair of infinitives (*agere et celerare* (line **9**) matches the subjunctives to present Agrippina's hasty action. That Lepida is swept aside so easily points to a woman versed in crime, and the reasoning of *muliebribus causis* (line **10**) is rich in meaning.

Lines 11–24

Narcissus enters the drama and thinks his doom is certain on account of his closeness and service to Claudius, but also because Lepida has met her end, whilst he suspects too much for his own good, and because he has no close association with either Nero or Britannicus. Suspecting Agrippina is plotting (**12–13**), and as the person who revealed Messalina's adulterous plotting to Claudius (**15–16**), Narcissus feels he too might be eliminated should the need arise—a suggestion all the more believable as a result of the fact that Tacitus leaves matters suitably vague, and because what is recorded is Narcissus' gossip with his closest associates (**12–13**). Agrippina and her lover, Pallas, are the new plotters in Narcissus' mind. The reference to Agrippina as *novercae* (**17**) may suggest that Narcissus does not dare utter her name through fear, but it also adds to the air of machination, and perhaps can be taken to suggest that Narcissus is gossiping pejoratively by not naming her. That Narcissus wishes he had kept his mouth shut about Messalina is highlighted by the dramatic description of the situation in which Narcissus now finds himself—the pejorative *novercae* (**17**), and the forceful *convelli* (**18**) present an imperial household being torn apart. The close repetition of *impudicitiam* (**18, 19**) shows that matters are just as bad, while the tricolon of *decus pudorem corpus* (**20**) stresses that power is all for Agrippina. The frequentative *dictitans* (**21**) combines with the *modo ... modo* (**22–23**) to reveal Narcissus' desperation when he addresses Britannicus, whilst the neat *patris ... matris ...* (**23–24**) not only makes his plea personal, but also reminds us that Narcissus has been using the term stepmother when talking with his cronies. The atmosphere of intrigue is all too apparent.

Lines 25–35

With Narcissus' convenient illness and absence (**25–26**), Agrippina acts. Whilst Narcissus is enjoying particularly pleasant surroundings (emphasised by the combination of *mollitia caeli et salubritate aquarum*: **26**), Agrippina's deeds seem all the more wicked, and the reader almost wonders whether the absence is enforced.

Agrippina's criminal powers are stressed—she has long been set on crime (*olim*: **27**) and now lacks no agents. Her deliberations are elegantly drawn out by Tacitus with *repentino et praecipiti* (**28–29**) nicely contrasted with *lentum et tabidum* (**29**) as she weighs up her options—heaven forbid that Claudius might actually live longer, find out, and thus prefer Britannicus! The chiastic arrangement of *turbaret ... differret* (**31–32**) allows us to see the dual purpose required by Agrippina of her rare potion, and so she grows in wickedness. The detail added in the brief character sketch of Locusta (**32–34**), Agrippina's new assistant, and the arrival in the plot of Halotus (**35**) add to the sense of drama.

Lines 36–44

The story, Tacitus remarks, is very well known—a situation emphasised by the use of *adeo*, *cuncta* and *pernotuere* (**36**). But Tacitus, with his masterful use of detail, tops the tale, allowing us to think that Claudius' own faults have their part to play in his demise. Lethargy or drunkenness (**38**) were involved, and the revelation of the lavatorial detail (**39**) not only points to Claudius' weakness but keeps the emperor alive that bit longer for Tacitus' sense of the dramatic. Agrippina might be terrified (**39**), but the quick introduction of the knowledge that a plan B (**41–43**) has been designed wipes out any possible thought of sympathy. The elegance of the parallel construction of passive infinitive followed by *cum* with a noun in the ablative (*incipi ... praemio*: **43–44**) points to Xenophon's greed but also serves to comment on the worse side of human nature—a habit Tacitus cannot resist.

Lines 45–54

There are many words of good intent, and Claudius' body is being wrapped up to supposedly aid his recovery whilst all is in hand to ensure Nero's succession (**45–48**). Agrippina feigns grief (*velut dolore victa*: **48**). The embracing of Britannicus (**49**) and the waylaying of Antonia and Octavia (**51**) reveal her unbridled wickedness but also her need to ensure the completion of the deed. The very mention of Chaldaean astrologers (**54**) adds to the drama of the occasion.

Lines 55–67

In whatever way, Claudius' death has now been achieved, and on 13 October Nero goes before the soldiers to win their support and be hailed as emperor (**55–57**). Tacitus would not have Nero have an easy ride, and it is only after the suggestion of the commander (*monente praefecto*: **57**) and the doubts of some (*dubitavisse quosdam*: **58**) that the soldiers settle for Hobson's choice (*mox nullo ... secuti sunt*: **59–60**). Divine honours (**64**) for Claudius are nothing new, and are very much a symbol of business as usual. The lack of reading of the will (**66**) allows affairs to die down, and a seemingly seamless transition to take effect.

Further teaching suggestions

- Ask students to construct a simple timeline of the events of the story.
- Have students produce a defence and prosecution speech for an imaginary prosecution of Agrippina.
- Following on from the activity above, study the passages from the *Pro Cluentio* which follow—what similarities are there between Agrippina and Sassia (in passage 2 below)?
- Create ideas about motives and characters using mind-mapping.
- Treat the story as a modern television detective might, with an incident board.
- Take this poisoning and use it for a longer project as part of a construction of a Roman boardgame based on 'Cluedo', complete with Latin room names for a Roman house (atrium, triclinium etc.) and appropriate weaponry.

Further reading

- The lives of the emperors generally, as written by Tacitus and Suetonius.
- Grant, Michael (trans.), *Tacitus: The Annals of Imperial Rome*, Penguin Classics, rev. edn (Harmondsworth: Penguin, 1989).
- Tingay, Graham (trans.), *Empire and Emperors: Selections from Tacitus' Annals*, Translations from Greek and Roman Authors (Cambridge: Cambridge University Press, 1983).
- Ash, Rhiannon, *Tacitus*, Ancients in Action (Bristol: Bristol Classical Press, 2006).
- Martin, Ronald, *Tacitus* (London: Bristol Classical Press, 1994).
- Kraus, C. S. and Woodman, A. J., *Latin Historians*, Greece & Rome New Surveys no. 27 (Oxford: Oxford University Press, 1997).
- Levick, Barbara, *Claudius* (New Haven: Yale University Press, 1990).
- Mellor, Ronald, *Tacitus* (New York: Routledge, 1993).
- Graves, Robert, I, *Claudius* (London: Barker, 1934) available in many more recent editions.
- Graves, Robert, *Claudius the God* (London: Barker, 1935) available in many more recent editions.
- The BBC adaptation of the Graves novels—*I, Claudius*.

2. The passion behind a trumped up charge of poison— Cicero *Pro Cluentio* 5.11–6.18 (abridged)

From his speech in defence of Aulus Cluentius, Cicero presents a picture of a woman driven by wicked passions and a son and daughter suffering as a result of those passions. Aulus Cluentius has been accused of poisoning (and murdering) Oppianicus, his mother Sassia's third husband. Oppianicus had previously tried to do the same to Cluentius and had been banished. His mother had attempted a similar prosecution to this one three years earlier, and Cluentius had been acquitted. Cicero succeeds in having Cluentius acquitted once more.

Themes for exploration

- Cicero's rhetorical style
- His character sketches
- Roman codes of right and wrong
- Morality and immorality
- The Roman family
- The excesses of passion

People and places

Aulus Cluentius (Minor)—the accused

Aulus Cluentius Habitus—father of the accused, who died in 88 BC, first husband of Sassia

Sassia—mother of the accused, who is behind this current prosecution

Melinus—Aulus Aurius Melinus, cousin and husband of Cluentia, daughter of Aulus Cluentius Habitus, second husband of Sassia

Cluentia—sister of the accused, first wife of Melinus

Oppianicus—third husband of Sassia, who allegedly attempted to kill Cluentius

Sulla—Lucius Cornelius Sulla Felix, a Roman general who twice marched on Rome, consul in 88 BC and 80 BC, and dictator 82–79 BC

Pompeius—Quintus Pompeius Rufus, consul with Sulla in 88 BC

Larinum—the town from which the family came (in the text Larinum is referred to by its adjective, *Larinas, -atis*).

Notes on text

Lines 1–22

Whilst we have a direct reference to the defendant (*huiusce*: **1**) as this passage opens, we also see a typical address to the judges of the case. The status and propriety of Aulus Cluentius Habitus are built up primarily by the *non solum ... sed etiam ...* construction (**1–2**), but also by the tricolon of ablatives praising his various qualities (**3**), and the delaying of *princeps* to the end of the sentence (**3**). Again, Cluentius is referred to as a fifteen-year-old when his father dies (**4**), and we see his sister quickly married to Melinus (**5–6**). Melinus' reputation is established by a quick description (*et honesto et nobili*: **7**), with the result that Sassia's wickedness, when it comes, will be even greater. Similarly the repetition of *plenae* (**8**) with regard to the quality and stability of their marriage allows even greater force to *repente* (**8**), and to the particularly strong vocabulary of *nefaria libido* (**9**). Not only that but Sassia is also described as *importunae* (**9**), and her lust is given further emphatic description (*non solum ... verum etiam ...*: **9–10**).

That Cicero emphasises how he will refer to Sassia as *mater* (**10–12**), whilst also highlighting her horrendous treatment of her son and daughter (*hostili odio et crudelitate*: **11**), marks out how she is acting in marked contrast with how a Roman *mater* should behave. The neat duo of *scelere et immanitate* (**13**) again stresses how wrong her passion is. Cicero then makes this point explicit and explains his reasoning. The pair of comparative adjectives (*amantiusque indulgentiusque*: **14**), followed by the juxtaposition of *filium interfectum* (**15–16**), ensure that we too, along with the jury, will consider that this singular crime is worthy of greater hatred (as directed by Cicero's address in the second person—*ducetis*: **17**). That her immoral (*contra quam fas*: **18**) passion cannot be contained for long adds speed to the narrative, whilst Cicero's imagery (*flagrare, inflammata*: **20**) is combined with the anaphora of *non* (**21–22**) and a great list of moral considerations which might be expected to exert some control in such a situation: nothing can hold her back.

Lines 23–38

The downfall of Melinus is hastened by the fact that the attributes of the age of wisdom, neatly expressed in *consilio ac ratione* (**23**), are not yet established. The strong *pellexit* (**23**) to express Sassia's actions is then followed by the more subtle *capi ac deleniri* (**24**). Cluentia very much is shown to be the wronged party, first by the simple reference to her as *filia* (**24**), and then by the exceptionally strong terms for her mother's actions (*nefarium paelicatum*: **26**). Not only does she face the pain that her husband is liaising with another woman (**25–26**)—but it is at the hands of her mother (**26**). The length of Cicero's sentence here not only serves to emphasise that Cluentia is the wronged party, but also reveals the shame she feels, together with the desperate nature of her grief and general situation (*maerore et lacrimis consenescebat*: **29**). The *ecce* (**29**) heralding the sudden divorce (**30**) highlights the scant consolation that this will bring: she does not want to lose her man (**32**). The sarcastic *egregia ac praeclara* (**32**), combined with the internal rhyme of *exsultare* and *triumphare*, lead us to the mocking title of *victrix* for Sassia (**33**)—yet, Cicero reminds us, she cannot control her passions. The ironic remark that Sassia did not want her reputation harmed (*laedi famam suam noluit*: **34–35**) not only mocks her but prepares us for the fact that we are going to be told of another outrageous deed: Sassia replaces her daughter in the marital bed (**35–37**). Her celebrations are told of by the pair of passive infinitives (*ornari et sterni*: **36**), and immediately we then see a pair of perfect passive participles to emphasise Sassia's treatment of Cluentia (*expulsa atque exturbata*: **36–37**). The unusual position of *nubit* (**37**) followed by the striking juxtaposition of *genero socrus* tells us all we need to know.

Lines 39–57

Cicero's strong exclamations are self-evident. The list of domestic (and marriage-related) items which Sassia did not fear emphasises the marital situation which she has spoilt, whilst the concessive *si minus ...* (**41**) allows us to recognise the contempt in which she holds the opinion of men and gods. Her utter destruction is expressed by the pair of strong verbs at the beginning of their sentence (*perfregit ac prostravit*: **44**), and her wild nature is similarly shown (*cupiditate atque furore*: **44**). Three nouns in the accusative demonstrating all the qualities Sassia should have are immediately followed by three abstract nouns in the nominative (**45**): her wild behaviour has won out. Her son Cluentius must bear not only the disgrace for the family (**45–46**), but also his sister's distress (**47–48**). He decides to do nothing more than refuse to treat Sassia as his mother, for fear that by doing so, he might legitimise her actions (**48–52**).

The long list of negatives (**53–54**) stresses the fact that Sassia is to blame for all her son's ills. Cicero then points out that Cluentius would supposedly have let bygones be bygones were it not for Sassia's further action against him (**55–57**).

Further teaching suggestions

- Remind students that this is actually a speech in defence of Cluentius—have them examine how he is portrayed, amidst such a scathing portrayal of Sassia.
- What similarities are there between Sassia and Agrippina (in passage 1 above)?
- Have students produce the story as it might be presented in a tabloid newspaper, ensuring that they pick out what the key facts are for themselves.

Further reading

- H. Grose-Hodge (ed.), *Cicero: Murder at Larinum: selections from the Pro Cluentio* (London: Bristol Classical Press, 1991).
- Translations of the speeches of Cicero (widely available).

● 3. A snake's poison stirs passion—Virgil *Aeneid* 7.341–372

Virgil's description of the passion caused by this snake entering Amata is vivid but also mysterious. The extract comes from Book 7 of the *Aeneid*, when the Trojans have landed in Italy and been welcomed by King Latinus. Latinus realises that Aeneas is the foreigner whom his daughter Lavinia is fated to marry. Juno, queen of the gods, is angered by the fact that the Trojans are prospering and therefore sends Allecto to cause trouble for the Trojans. Consequently, Amata's hatred for Aeneas and the Trojans develops rapidly and violently, but the exact movements of the snake are not always clear.

Themes for exploration

- Virgil's descriptive language
- Snakes as symbols of evil
- Amata's rhetoric

Metre—Hexameters

People and places

Amata—queen of Latium, wife of King Latinus, king of the Laurentines and ruler of Latium

Lavinia—daughter of Latinus and Amata

Latium—coastal area of Italy south of the River Tiber

Laurentum—the capital of Latium

Allecto—one of the Furies.

Gorgoneus—of the Gorgons: Allecto has snakes for her hair like the Gorgon, Medusa.

Teucri—another name for the Trojans (Teucer was an ancient king of Troy)

Turnus—prince of the Rutulians, a neighbouring people, who has been seen as a likely candidate for marriage to Lavinia

Phrygius—Phrygian, synonymous with Trojan in the *Aeneid*

Aquilo—the North wind

Lacedaemon—Sparta was otherwise known as Lacedaemon

Leda—mother of Helen, and wife of Tyndareus

Helen—wife of Menelaus, king of Sparta, abducted by Paris thus beginning the Trojan War; daughter of Zeus and Leda

Faunus—father of King Latinus, who has told him that Lavinia is fated to marry a foreigner

Inachus—king of Argos in Greece, and father of Io

Acrisius—king of Argos, and father of Danae

Mycenae—city in the Argolid in Greece

Notes on text

Lines 1–18

The picture of Allecto's poison is made more evil by *Gorgoneis* (**1**), whilst *exim* (**1**) indicates her speed in seeking out Amata amidst silence (**2–3**). The scene is thus set. Amata already has the stirrings of hatred against the Trojans as the harsh internal rhyme of *curaeque iraeque* (**5**) indicates. Nor is *coquebant* (**5**) entirely without a pejorative touch. It is only fitting therefore that a fairly grim goddess is pulling the strings: the dark *caeruleis ... crinibus* (**6**) and the force of *conicit* (**7**) add to that grim portrayal. The snake is inserted deep within Amata as the seventh line of the extract emphasises. Amata will cause mayhem as both *omnem* and *permisceat* suggest (line **8**).

The snake moves within her clothes, without Amata feeling it (**9–10**), and becomes part of her very being, mental and physical. Mysteriously it can breathe its spirit into her (**11**). The repetition of *fit* (**11–12**) ensures that it becomes part of Amata's physical adornment, and there is not a little hint of menace in its wanderings (*membris lubricus errat*: **13**). Its gradual movement is reinforced by *sublapsa*, and *lues* and *veneno* together emphasise the strength of its effects (**14**), but at first she speaks in a gentle fashion (**17**).

Lines 19–32

Her words (**19–26**) are directed at Latinus, and she questions him about the marriage-worthiness of Aeneas, attempting to engender his pity with the repetition of *miseret* (**20, 21**). There is plentiful alliteration to add force to her words, and the choice of *perfidus ... praedo* (**22**) is particularly effective. The reference to the situation of Helen (**24**) is fitting for her role in causing the Trojans' present situation. Amata then with two questions appeals to the sacred pledge which Latinus has made betrothing Lavinia to Turnus (**25–26**). Changing tack slightly, she then tries to assert that Turnus is the foreigner desired by the oracle (**27–30**), citing his Greek origins (**31–32**)—appropriately enough for an enemy of the Trojans.

> ### Further teaching suggestions
>
> - A quick read of *Aeneid* 2 in translation will provide more epic snake images (similes). Use these together with other images to see what Virgil is trying to convey here.
>
> - It is important that students place this passage in its context—provide a timeline of the *Aeneid* up to this point, or have students produce their own.
>
> - 🔊 Listen to the passages on the audio CD (tracks 17–18)—how does Virgil use sound to create an appropriately menacing atmosphere?

> ### Further reading
>
> - Fordyce, C. (ed.), *Virgil: Aeneid VII & VIII* (London: Bristol Classical Press, 1991).
>
> - *The Cambridge Companion to Virgil*, ed. Charles Martindale (Cambridge: Cambridge University Press, 1997).
>
> - Translations of the *Aeneid* (widely available).

4. Medea's impassioned plea to Jason—Ovid *Heroides* 12.160–213

This extract from Ovid's *Heroides* allows students to witness the passionate character that is Medea before she enacts her revenge upon Jason and his new love. She is also someone who is very much involved in poisons. Ovid's *Heroides* consists of a series of letters by various leading ladies from the world of classical mythology to their respective husbands or lovers. Ovid's sense of exaggeration is never far away. His dramatic portrayal of Medea here is all the more important for the fact that his tragedy, *Medea*, has not survived.

Themes for exploration

- Medea's passionate language and the actual arguments she uses
- Marriage in the ancient world
- The role of children in the ancient world
- The Medea myth
- Revenge
- Sympathy for Medea/Jason

Metre—Elegiacs

People and places

Aeetes—Medea's father, king of Colchian Aia

Glauke—Jason's new love

Creon—Glauke's father and king of Corinth

Colchis—kingdom on the eastern shores of the Black Sea

Hecate—goddess of witchcraft and the Underworld

Tyrius—Tyrian (of the rich colour, Tyrian purple)

Graius—Greek

Sisyphius—of Sisyphus, and therefore unending or pointless: the punishment of Sisyphus was unending

Notes on text

Lines 1–24

The extract begins with an acknowledgement from Medea for the wrongs she has done her father and native land through *laese* and *relicti* (**1**), as well as the series of imperatives telling of her real emotion at this point (**1–2**). However, those commands to her father, native land and shades of her brother are quickly dealt with and Medea moves to her own problems (*deseror amissis*: **3**) as opposed to what she had done to them. In lines **4–5**, Medea vividly shows with her *potui/non potui* contrast the power Jason has had over her, and her knowledge of potions has no effect on the flames of her own passion. She too is now abandoned by all her powers (**9–10**), and the repetitive *–que* is then picked up in line **10** by the repetition of *nil*. The contrasting juxtaposition of *dies noctes* in line **11** emphasises how little sleep Medea is allowed in her state of passion for Jason, whilst line **13** again shows the contrast between her powers in general and her ability to use them in her own situation.

Line **15** sees Medea focus on the physical nature of Jason, and she uses the harsh *paelex* to describe her love-rival Glauke. The insults then continue with *stultae* and *iniustis* on lines **17** and **18**, as Medea imagines Jason and his new lover scheming against her. The veiled threat behind the repetition of the subjunctive *rideat* (**20, 21**) is soon followed by the future tenses of *flebit* and *vincet* (**22**): Medea will use every method against her enemy, including poison (**23–24**).

Lines 25–54

From talking about Glauke, Medea moves back to a very direct message for Jason, casting herself in the role of suppliant, reminding Jason of his previous need for assistance from her (*quam tu mihi saepe fuisti*: **27**). The *si* clauses on lines **25** and **29** are persuasive, and the second on line **29** allows the focus to fall on their children. Medea's very particular worries come in the harsh *saeviet* and *dira noverca* on line **30**. The repetition of *per* on lines **33** and **34** stresses her emotion, and is followed by a string of requests (*redde, adde, refer*: **35–36**). The vocabulary of line **37** returns to the vocabulary of the earlier part of this extract, and the volume of personal pronouns referring to the pair of them allows Medea to build up to the juxtaposition *parente parens* on line **40**: they became parents together.

Medea's question on line **41** continues to show her anger and reminds us of Jason's past deeds in her native land. She equates her dowry (*dos mea*: **44**, **45**) with the safety of Jason and that of his crew—that is what kept them alive. As result he now has not only his life, but also a bride and powerful father-in-law—whether current or future (**47**). She breaks off to ask a rhetorical question (**49–50**). The repetition of *ira* (**50, 51**) shows her strength of feeling and begins to indicate that she will move beyond threats (**54**). Medea will go on to provide Glauke with a poisoned crown and robe which will kill her. She then kills her children.

Further teaching suggestions

- 🔊 Listen to the passage on the audio CD (tracks 19–20). How does Ovid recreate an aural picture of Medea's passion?
- This extract might provide ideal practice for those attempting some Latin reading aloud—ask your students to attempt their own version.
- Explore the Medea story in other authors.
- Ask your students to assess how convincing Medea's arguments are.

Further reading

- Knox, Peter E. (ed.), *Ovid, Heroides: Select Epistles*, Cambridge Greek and Latin Classics (Cambridge: Cambridge University Press, 1996).
- Lively, Genevieve, *Ovid: Love Song*, Ancients in Action (Bristol: Bristol Classical Press, 2005).
- Armstrong, Rebecca, *Ovid and His Love Poetry*, Classical Literature and Society (London: Duckworth, 2005).
- Fulkerson, Laurel, *The Ovidian Heroine as Author: Reading, Writing, and Community in the Heroides* (Cambridge: Cambridge University Press, 2005).
- *The Cambridge Companion to Ovid*, ed. Philip Hardie (Cambridge: Cambridge University Press, 2002).

🔊 5. Catullus struggles with love—Catullus 76 ad deos

This poem comes towards the end of the love affair of Catullus and Lesbia. He has been a faithful lover to her, but now he must get over his love. It is thought Lesbia (a name she acquires most probably through poem 51) was the notorious Clodia, sister of Publius Clodius Pulcher, the rabble-rousing politician (see Section 2.8), and wife of Quintus Caecilius Metellus Celer.

Themes for exploration

- Love and Catullus' affair with Lesbia
- Religious and financial imagery
- The heightened emotional and personal language
- Catullus' personal mental struggle and the poem's focus on Catullus himself
- Advice for other people

Metre—Elegiacs

Notes on text

The idea that Catullus expects something in return for his previous good deeds (**1**) is all too soon apparent. It quickly becomes clear that although Catullus may begin by writing of men in general, it is he who has done good things in the past to the gods and therefore feels justified in expecting good things in the years to come (**5**). He has been dutiful (**3**), he has not violated any sacred pledge (**3**), nor broken any oath to deceive men (**4**), and yet there are signs that his affair with Lesbia is not all he wants it to be (*ingrato amore*: **6**). As well as the religious references, *credita* and *perierunt* on line **9** may suggest financial imagery adding weight to Catullus' idea of wanting something in return. This is elaborated in lines **7** and **8** where *dicere* and *facere* are picked up by *dictaque factaque*—Catullus has said and done everything he should, so why is it all going wrong?

The questions which follow are made emphatic by a variety of factors: the choice and position of *excrucies* on line **10**; the three verbs in the second person singular; the personal pronouns and the position of *miser* (**11–12**). Catullus must use such strong language to show the mental struggle he faces—as Quinn suggests, this poem is not quite at the end of the affair, and lines **12–14** clearly illustrate that that end for Catullus is a difficult one. Students' attention should be drawn to the repetition of *difficile* (**13, 14**) and *hoc* (**15, 16**), the iussive subjunctives of *efficias* (**14**) and *facias* (**16**) ('you must effect/do this') and the very strong (dispondaic) *pervincendum* (gerundive of obligation), as well as *una salus* (**15**): and the rather emphatic *sive id non pote sive pote* (**16**).

Lines **17–26** represent a final prayer of pleading by Catullus, beginning with two *si* clauses (**17–18**), followed by an imperative (*aspicite*: **19**), another *si* clause (**19**), and another imperative (*eripite*: **20**), and an explanation of Catullus' state of misery.

There is obvious alliteration (*me miserum, pestem perniciemque* (**19, 20**)—the latter also being an example of hendiadys) emphasising Catullus' strength of feeling and his emotion, a reminder of the beginning of the poem (*vitam puriter egi*: **19**) as well as the portrayal of the emotional and physical effects of this love being combined. Catullus makes it clear that he is not seeking the impossible (*non ... quaero*: **23**) and gives a clear indication of what he wants (*opto*: **25**), picking up on the language he has used earlier in the poem (*deponere*: **13**), before finishing with another imperative (*reddite*: **26**) which returns us to the idea fleshed out in lines **1–9**.

Further teaching suggestions

- Ask your students to construct an advice page of a modern magazine detailing both Catullus' letter to the magazine, and the agony aunt/uncle's reply.
- Collect Latin examples of how forceful Catullus' language is in this poem.

Further reading

- Catullus poems 8 and 51 (see section 2.2b and 2.2c)—the latter uses some similar language.
- Catullus poem 72 (which follows: section 3.6).
- Quinn, Kenneth (ed.), *Catulllus, The Poems*, rev. edn (London: Bristol Classical Press, 1996).
- Translations of the poems of Catullus (widely available).
- Wiseman, T. P., *Catullus and his World* (Cambridge: Cambridge University Press, 1985).
- Hurley, Amanda Kolson, *Catullus*, Ancients in Action (Bristol: Bristol Classical Press, 2004).

6. Passion fades—Catullus 72

There is a certain world-weary tone to Catullus' words here. He is now experienced in his affair with Lesbia and knows all too well the changing fortunes of love.

Metre—Elegiacs

Notes on text

The imperfect *dicebas* (**1**) almost pre-empts what comes in line **5**: things are no longer what they were. Catullus was her everything and her only love (**1–2**)—or so she claimed. His love for her used to be also like that of a father (**4**)—perhaps believing his children can do no wrong—but the situation has changed as the bitterness of line **5** reveals. Catullus is still impassioned (**5**), but Lesbia is cheaper and more fickle (**6**). The neat word order of the last line presents this lover's paradox extremely well.

7. The passions of a ghostly fury—Ovid *Ibis* 133–158 (abridged)

These lines from Ovid's *Ibis* form part of his vicious attack on an unknown enemy, who is referred to by the title of the poem (named after the bird, the ibis). The poem is thought to have its origins in a lost work of Callimachus.

Metre—Elegiacs

People and places

Thraces—the Thracians, from northern Greece

Iazyges—the Iazyges, a tribe from the Black Sea coast

Ganges—the River Ganges in India

Hister—the River Danube in mainland Europe

Tiberis—the River Tiber in Rome

Tuscus—Tuscan or Etruscan (of that area of Italy north of the River Tiber)

Manes—the spirits of the Underworld

Stygius—of the River Styx; river of the Underworld, on the shores of which souls of men waited before crossing over on Charon's ferryboat

Notes on text

Whatever the circumstances, Ovid is clear that he will torment the man whom he hates, and will wage war against him. This is made most clear through the series of contrasts presented in the first four lines, amidst some neat chiasmus in line **1** (*arcu ... hasta*) and a series of direct antitheses in lines **2–3**. The death of either man will not bring an end to such anger, and the juxtaposition (*in Manes Manibus*) of line **6** is striking. The idea of *vacuas ... in auras* (**7**) is picked up by *exsanguis ... umbra* (**8**), whilst the repetition of *tum quoque* (**7, 9**) stresses that there will be no let-up once Ovid has died. The all encompassing *quicquid ero* (**11**) emphasises this, and the number of verbs in the first person singular (**11–16**) show that Ovid's ghostly fury may have cold hands (**12**), but his passion burns. We may note sibilance particularly in lines **13** and **14** adding to the poet's menaces. The verbs *cernes* (**13**) and *ages* (**15**) are quickly followed up again by threats from Ovid of what he will do. Lines **17** and **18** finish the extract with a horrid image, and harsh assonance.

Further teaching suggestions

- Listen to the extract on the audio CD (track 23). What aspects of Ovid's language convey the poet's need for revenge?

Further reading

- Ellis, Robinson (ed.), *Ovid: Ibis*, new edn (Exeter: Bristol Phoenix Press, 2008; originally published by Oxford University Press, 1881).
- *The Cambridge Companion to Ovid*, ed. Philip Hardie (Cambridge: Cambridge University Press, 2002).

4 LAND AND SEA

Contents overview

Prose

1. A governor travels to his province: Pliny *Letters*
2. The army on land and sea
   a. A difficult landing: Caesar *Gallic war*
   b. Land and sea confused: Tacitus *Annals*
3. Hannibal crosses the Alps: Livy *A History of Rome*

🔊 **Verse**

4. A traveller's tales: Horace *Satires*
5. A storm at sea: Virgil *Aeneid*
6. The ship of state in troubled waters: Horace *Odes*

Themes in this section

Travel by land	1, 2a, 3, 4
Travel by sea	1, 2b, 5, 6

The army	2a and b, 3
Travel for work	1, 4
Discomforts of travel, illness	1, 4
Fear or suspicion of the sea	2a and b, 5
Death by drowning compared unfavourably with death in battle	2b, 5
Bad weather, storms, problems with tides	*passim*
Sea travel as allegory	6
The sea and the gods	5, 6
Stylistic features in description of land and sea:	
mock epic	4
metrical effects	5
personification	2b, 4, 5
word order	5

1. A governor travels to his province—Pliny *Letters* 10

Pliny's correspondence with the emperor Trajan over the two years of his appointment as governor with special powers in Bithynia and Pontus provides an insight into Roman provincial government—a combination of delegated authority and consultation, local knowledge, flexibility and initiative, and a desire to be both firm and fair. (For a very different, corrupt provincial governor see Cicero's portrait of Verres, section 1.5.) Here we see Pliny at the very beginning of his assignment, ensuring that Trajan is kept informed of his whereabouts and progress on an arduous journey that took about six weeks.

Themes for exploration

- The provincial governor
- Difficulties of travel
- Travel for work: modes of transport

People and places

Pliny—Gaius **Plinius** Caecilius Secundus, AD 61/62–*c*.113, known as Pliny the Younger; his correspondence with the emperor Trajan from his province is the source for much of our knowledge of how Roman provinces were managed.

Trajan—Marcus Ulpius Trajanus, emperor AD 98–117; his letters to Pliny reveal him as a moderate ruler.

Ephesus—city in Roman province of Asia (now modern Turkey)

Malea—the southern tip of the Peloponnese, a dangerous stretch of water owing to changes in wind direction

Pergamum—an important city in Mysia (Asia Minor)

Bithynia—a Roman province on the south coast of the Black Sea, administered together with Pontus

Prusenses—people of Prusa, a city in Bithynia

Notes on text

(Letters 15, 16 and 17a)

15.1, 16.1, 17.1 Forms of address. Pliny addresses the emperor as *domine*. This is probably used as the natural way in which a lesser or junior official would address his superiors. It is not exclusive to emperors, and the early emperors in particular avoided it as sounding too tyrannical. In his reply, Trajan uses the familiar, personal vocative *mi Secunde carissime*, as he does often though not in every letter.

15.1–2 Pliny expects (rightly, judging by Trajan's reply) that his progress will be of concern to the emperor (*ad curam tuam pertinere* 15.1 and *pertinet ad animum meum* 16.1–2). In line 1 (*confido ... pertinere*), supply *hoc* to complete the accusative and infinitive construction.

15.3 *hyper Malean*. The southern tip of the Peloponnese. The phrase referring to this place, notorious as a meeting-point of conflicting prevailing winds, appears in Greek in Pliny's letter, perhaps because of its proverbial reputation: there was a Greek saying 'Round Malea and forget your folks at home'.

15.4–6 and **17a.5** *contrariis ventis*. The more general problems of contrary winds and trade winds at particular seasons. These problems were aggravated by the fact that Pliny was sailing late in the season, either because his predecessor had died in office and had to be replaced quickly, or because his departure was delayed by his own illness. See Sherwin-White pp. 581, 582.

15.4–5 and **17a.3–6** The perennial decision of whether to travel by ship or land.

15.6 *sicut ... ita ... . sicut* in conjunction with *ita* here means 'while' or 'although'. *ita* is not translated separately. The same construction appears in 10.17a lines 2–3.

15.6 *continuae ... reluctantur. continuae* could be either dative with *navigationi* or nominative plural with *etesiae*.

17a.2–3 See above on *sicut ... ita .... expertus* needs to be translated as *expertus sum*. Pliny's pause at Pergamum, to the north and inland from Ephesus, is surprising. He apparently started on the land route, but the fever, heat and discomfort persuaded him to head for the coast and take the sea route instead. Pliny wants both to explain his later arrival, but also to play down his illness with the diminutive *febriculis*.

17a.8 *natalem tuum*. This fell the day after Pliny's arrival, allowing him to present his late arrival in a positive light .

17a.9–13 As his senatorial career had included posts with financial responsibility, a major part of Pliny's brief was to regularise the management of public money. He immediately began his inspections in order to eliminate embezzlement and unnecessary or irregular expenditure.

Further teaching suggestions

Content

- What problems and hazards of travel by land and sea does Pliny mention? What other difficulties might travel by sea and by land have involved, other than the ones Pliny mentions? Present the factors Pliny had to take into account in a table:

Travel by land	For	Against

Travel by sea	For	Against

- In the light of Pliny's journey, his arrival and the start of his work, compare him with a modern diplomat or business executive travelling, arriving and working abroad. What are the similarities and differences?

Style

- Some points could be brought out by reading the letters aloud, different students taking the parts of Pliny and Trajan.
- In 10.17a, how does Pliny use superlatives to add to the impact of his letter?
- In his replies to Pliny's letters, Trajan often uses the same or similar words. How does *Letter* 10.16 illustrate this?
- How is the difference in status between Pliny and Trajan reflected in the style of the letters?

Further reading

- Williams, W. (ed.), *Pliny the Younger: Correspondence with Trajan from Bithynia* (*Epistles X*), Parallel Latin text and translation, commentary (Oxford: Aris and Phillips, 1990).
- Sherwin-White, A. N. (ed.), *The Letters of Pliny: A Social and Historical Commentary* (Oxford: Oxford University Press, 1966). A large and thorough work, with articles on key aspects of Pliny's letters, including the correspondence with Trajan, which has informed subsequent studies but is useful to consult on points of detail.
- Radice, B. (trans.), *The Letters of the Younger Pliny*, Penguin Classics, rev. repr. (Harmondsworth, Penguin, 1969).
- Walsh, P. G., (trans.), *Pliny the Younger: Complete Letters*, Oxford World's Classics (Oxford, Oxford University Press 2006).

2. The army on land and sea

In both of these passages we see the Roman army coping with unfamiliar terrain and treacherous seas.

a. A difficult landing—Caesar *Gallic War* 4.23–26 (abridged)

Throughout this passage there are contrasts between the Romans' unfamiliarity with the place and the Britons' familiarity, between the advantage of the enemy position and the disadvantage of the Romans'. The other point of interest is how the Roman response to the situation is described.

Themes for exploration
- Fear of the sea
- View of the enemy
- Military discipline: the use of symbols such as the standard, colours
- Style: a campaign diary

People and places

Julius Caesar—Gaius Julius Caesar, 100–44 BC, first invaded Britain from the Roman province of Gaul in 55 BC.

Volusenus—a military tribune serving under Caesar

Notes on text

Lines 1–8

This section can serve as an introduction to Caesar's compact, business-like style, manifested conspicuously in the use of participles in phrases or specifically in ablative absolutes:

participles: *arbitratus* (1); *nactus* (6); *progressus* (8)

ablative absolutes: *legatis ... convocatis* (3); *his dimissis* (6); *dato ... ancoris* (7)

These and other examples in the following sections will sometimes need to be rendered as main clauses to break up long sentences.

1 *nequaquam idoneum locum*. An understatement, as it was the rain of enemy missiles just mentioned that made the place unsuitable.

5 *monuitque ... administrarentur*. A parenthesis (omitted) spells out the unpredictability of

sea-battles as a particular reason for promptness in obeying orders in warfare.

8 *aperto ... litore*. i.e. away from the cliffs, at Lympne or between Walmer Castle and Deal further along the coast.

Lines 9–21

Caesar describes the Romans' disadvantages and the Britons' advantages.

9–10 *praemisso ... essedariis*. *praemisso* agrees with *equitatu* but applies also to *essedariis*.

12–13 *quod naves ... non poterant*. Caesar may have succeeded in bringing some ships to land (line 10 above), but once the Britons had occupied the beach, he had to resort to mooring them in the deeper water.

13–16 *militibus autem ... pugnandum*. The dative *militibus* (qualified by the phrase *magno ... oppressis*), with the gerundives *desiliendum*, and *consistendum* and *pugnandum*, needs to be distinguished from the ablatives in the ablative absolutes *ignotis ... manibus*. The threefold list of hindrances suffered by the Romans is matched by the three things they have to do in spite of the hindrances.

16–19 *cum illi ... incitarent*. Making a list of the enemy's advantages, parallel to the Romans' disadvantages, is a way of showing how the advantages are listed in reverse order: **unknown territory**—underlined encumbered—**waves; dry land or shallow water**—underlined unencumbered—**very familiar territory**. The verbs of the *cum* clause, *conicerent* and *incitarent*, indicate that the enemy are already fighting, while for the Romans, still struggling to disembark, engagement is still a task that lies ahead, expressed in the gerundives. In translation, the long sentence will need breaking up, but students can also appreciate how it enables the series of contrasts to be made.

20 *alacritate ac studio.* The usual hallmarks of Caesar's troops.

Lines 22–30

The team spirit of the Roman forces and the power of the military standards are dramatically demonstrated.

22 *cunctantibus.* The delay was particularly dangerous now as the Romans risked losing the temporary advantage they had gained from the withdrawal of the enemy from the Roman war machines.

24–25 *nisi … prodere.* The loss of a legion's eagle or other standards was a massive humiliation. In a disastrous engagement with German tribes under Varus (AD 9), the Romans lost the eagle

and standards. Varus took his own life, and troops and commanders were massacred by the enemy. Tacitus describes the recovery of the eagle of the 19th brigade and Germanicus' visit to the site of the catastrophe (*Annals* 1.60–61). Here the man's gesture and his words encourage the men not to be outdone by one of their number and to be loyal to the army (embodied in the eagle), their commander and the state.

Lines 31–35

After some disarray in disembarking, the Roman forces act true to form.

31 *in arido.* At last the Romans enjoyed the right conditions for battle.

32–35 *neque … defuit.* The successful engagement is not to be confused with victory. Without the cavalry to pursue the enemy, Caesar could not gain a hold and because the sailing season was coming to an end he had to sail immediately.

b. Land and sea confused—Tacitus *Annals* 1.70

An incident from the campaign of Germanicus, general and nephew of the emperor Tiberius. A prudent lightening of the ships has near-catastrophic results as a high tide, made higher by strong winds, turns land to sea and engulfs the troops.

Themes for exploration
- Unpredictability of sea; fear of death at sea
- Great escapes
- Style: polished history; contrast

People and places

Germanicus/Germanicus Caesar—Nero Claudius Germanicus (15/16 BC–AD 19), nephew of the emperor Tiberius. When Tiberius adopted him as his son, he took the name Germanicus Julius Caesar. As a general he led campaigns in Gaul and Germany.

Publius Vitellius—a trusted commander, fought with Germanicus in Gaul and Germany

Lines 1–6

This first section describes the rapid reversal of fortune of the troops on the land.

1 *at Germanicus. at* marks the return to the main narrative of Germanicus' movements.

2–3 *quo … levior. levior* here is used predicatively, and is best translated as an adverb. Germanicus wanted to lighten the load of the ships so that they would stay afloat, or float more lightly, in shallow water, whether they were navigating in shallow water or were grounded at low tide and needed to float off more readily. The problem arose from the low tides found around the estuary of the river Ems (off the north coast of modern Germany).

3–6 *Vitellius … agmen.* In the space of a sentence, Tacitus paints a picture of a straightforward, peaceful march on dry land, followed immediately by the opposite picture of the attack of wind and tide on the troops. The contrast is achieved by the content and poetic touches (e.g. *inpulsu aquilonis*, 5). Publius Vitellius, who fought with Germanicus in Gaul and Germany, was the uncle of Vitellius, emperor in AD 69. *sidere aequinoctii*. Germanicus was heading for home as the autumn equinox, notorious for high winds and tides, marked the end of the campaigning season.

Lines 7–14

In a series of unconnected sentences (asyndeton), Tacitus describes the overwhelming of the troops by the sea. Students might notice the striking lack of conjunctions after the initial *et*.

7–8 *opplebantur … a profundis*. The covering of the land is illustrated in the description of the sameness of sea, shore and fields, and the lack of distinctions in the terrain. *brevia* in the sense of shallows is poetic (cf. passage 4.5 'A storm at sea' line 31).

8–14 *sternuntur … involvebantur*. Within the indiscriminate **drowning** of the troops, there is a movement from **general loss and disaster** (*sternuntur … occursant*), through the **breakdown of formation** (*permiscentur … obruti*) to the **annihilation of mutual support** and the **levelling of capabilities and strategies** in the **universal disaster** (*non vox … involvebantur*).

Lines 15–22

They pass a miserable night on higher ground. The tide is down by morning, and they are picked up by Germanicus.

15 *eodem*. Indicates concisely that the scattered troops were reunited.

17–19 *haud minus … exitium*. For the sentiment see passage 4.5 'A storm at sea' where Aeneas exclaims at the good fortune of those killed in battle at Troy compared with his own likely death at sea (lines 14–21).

19 *lux*. A poetic personification.

20–21 *vagante … submersas*. The rumour underlines both the severity of the catastrophe and the scale of their deliverance.

Further teaching suggestions

Content

- Make a list of the similarities and differences between the difficulties the sea caused in the two passages.

- In each passage the Romans are in difficulties but they escape from them. What difference would it have made if the author had played down the dangers instead of describing them vividly? Consider the impact of both the dangers and the escape from them.

- Which passage would you choose to make into a film sequence, and why?

Style

- Try rewriting (in English) the first paragraph of passage b as Caesar might have described it.

- In what ways is passage b more poetic?

Further reading

- John, D., *Caesar: 55 and 54 BC Expeditions to Britain*, Latin Texts (London: Bristol Classical Press/Duckworth 1991).

- Hammond, C. (trans.), *Caesar: The Gallic War*, Oxford World's Classics (Oxford: Oxford University Press 1996).

- Miller, N. P., *Tacitus: Annals Book I* (London, Methuen 1959; repr. London, Bristol Classical Press/Duckworth 1989). Text, commentary and vocabulary.

- Grant, M. (trans.), *Tacitus: The Annals of Imperial Rome*, rev edn (Harmondsworth: Penguin Classics, 1989).

3. Hannibal crosses the Alps—Livy *A History of Rome* 21

An extract from Livy's account of the Carthaginian leader's campaign against Rome in the Second Punic War. An extract from Juvenal *Satires* 10 sums up the boldness of Hannibal's crossing of the Alps in order to invade Italy: 'Nature blocks his way with the Alps and with snow: he splits boulders and breaks open a mountain with vinegar!' (lines 152–153).

Themes for exploration

- Animals in ancient warfare
- An army on the march
- Dangers of mountain travel
- Leadership qualities

People and places

Alps—the mountain range crosses northern Italy

Hannibal—247–183/182 BC, a Carthaginian general who led his troops into Italy over the Alps in 218 BC

Vergiliae—the Pleiades, a constellation

Po Valley—flat lands around the river Po (*Circumpadani* in the text)

New Carthage—in Latin Carthago Nova, a city with a fine harbour founded by Hannibal's brother Hasdrubal on the south coast of Spain; now known as Cartagena

Notes on text

Lines 1–4

Hannibal's elephants

1–3 *elephanti … praebebant.* The awkwardness of the elephants on the pass is compensated for by the fear they spread among the enemy. *elephanti* is subject of *praebebant.*

4 *perventum est.* A common formation of the perfect tense in Livy. It will be met again in lines 25 *ventum* (*est*), 47 *descensum* (*est*) and 49 *perventum est.*

Lines 5–17

To troops worn out and terrified by snow Hannibal points out the vista of Italy from the summit.

5 *labore ac pugnando.* The effort of the climb, and the need to fight off a serious ambush from the native population on the way up.

8 *occidente…Vergiliarum.* The setting of the Pleiades marked the onset of winter, so it is probably used here in that sense rather than of a particular date. This first fall of snow was unseasonable; it usually occurred in late September, when Hannibal was coming to the end of his crossing.

9 *ingentem terrorem.* The emotion of southern peoples confronted by snow for the first time in an already hostile environment.

9–10 *signis … motis.* The phrase *prima luce*, enclosed in the ablative absolute *signis … motis* indicates when the column got under way.

14 *transcendere.* Roman historians regularly used speeches to convey arguments or feelings at a particular moment: Hannibal may or may not have made this particular speech at this juncture but it effectively sums up the situation and is a much-needed encouragement to men in their desperate state. The present infinitive encourages the soldiers to see themselves in their imaginations crossing the Italian fortifications at that very moment, not in the future.

15–17 *cetera … habituros.* Later events prove this to have been a wildly optimistic if inspirational calculation. He was a real threat to Rome but his advance was resisted and despite inflicting conspicuous defeats on the Romans, the worst being at Cannae in 216, he was defeated by Scipio Africanus in 202.

16–17 *in manu ac potestate.* A legal expression derived from marriage.

17 *habituros.* In view of Hannibal's upbeat speech, 'about to hold' would be a suitable translation.

Lines 18–41

The descent, bringing the first indications that the remainder of the journey was not in fact going to be straightforward. At least they are not harassed by the enemy to the same extent as on the ascent.

20–21 *ut ... sunt*. This is actually the case.

25 *ad ... rupem*. Below (line 28) Livy describes the place being naturally steep, but the narrowness of the path and the precipice falling away from it may have been due to earlier landslides. Livy envisages a landslide ahead of the troops, so that the path narrows to nothing above the sheer drop.

26 *expeditus miles*. The meaning is that even a lightly-armed soldier would have difficulty, let alone a whole marching column encumbered with equipment and baggage animals, not to mention elephants.

32–34 *tandem ... fuit*. Having prevented a successful detour, the snow now hampers the process of making a camp.

35–39 *inde ... putrefaciunt*. A long sentence that will need breaking up by ending sentences at *ducti* (*sunt*) and *faciunt*, with the possibility of rendering the participles in the ablative absolutes as active finite verbs. The force of *et* in line 38 (*et vis venti*) is 'also': the force of the wind was *also* necessary.

39 *ardentiaque ... pandunt*. Juvenal's reference makes clear that this incident was legendary, but it is difficult to see how sheer perpendicular rocks could have been subjected to this treatment effectively, though it may have been possible to soften the rock if not actually split it. Polybius, who also describes Hannibal's crossing and followed Hannibal's route over the Alps himself, does not mention the process and envisages a different lie of the land. This does not mean that Hannibal did not use the process at any point: it is attested in Latin literature as a mining technique (e.g. Pliny the Elder *Natural History* 33.71 describes the process as a possible method for breaking through flint in Spanish gold mines), and Livy's description here is a vivid illustration of the kind of hazards that Hannibal would have met and the ingenuity with which he would have dealt with them. (See Walsh pp. 192ff.) In his translation de Sélincourt assumes

that the vinegar is 'the men's rations of sour wine'. Whether vinegar would have been more effective than any cold liquid is debatable (see **www.unc. edu/~duncan/personal/roman_mining/deep-vein_mining.htm** 'Underground workings'), but in any case it was probably the only liquid they had.

40–41 *molliuntque ... possent*. Again, it is hard to envisage even a zigzag causeway being constructed if the rock was as perpendicular as implied in lines 25–29, but it was a familiar engineering ploy to ease the gradient (Caesar describes a steep road to a town in Gaul as being made easier by zigzags, *Gallic War* 7.46.2) so Roman readers would have recognised it as a means of tackling the kind of problem Hannibal would have met in the Alps.

ut ... possent. The completion of the road brings the reversal of the situation in 26, the end of an accumulation of hardships starting at line 25: **impassable precipice—abortive detour—fatigue** brought on by **snow** on journey and when pitching camp—**effort of constructing road** over precipice—**passable road completed**.

Lines 42–51

At last, the prospect of the ease promised in line 15 as Hannibal completes the crossing.

42 *quadriduum ... consumptum*. Indicates the speed of the operation to build the road.

44–48 *inferiora ... ingeniis*. In three short sentences, the troops leave the peaks and recover from their crossing of the Alps in the lands below, perhaps Alpine pastures, rather than the plain which is reached later (line 47 *ad planum descensum*). In lines 44–45 the accumulation of the pleasing features that these lands have conveys their abundance, and provides a strong contrast with the inhospitableness of the mountain peaks with their snow and hard labour.

45 *et iam ... loca*. In apposition to and summing up the features of the landscape in lines 43-44, emphasised by *et iam* ('in fact', cf. line 47).

45–47 *ibi ... data*. Instead of describing the descent of Hannibal and his troops, Livy emphasises its speed and ease by merely stating their enjoyment of the lands into which they have descended.

47–48 *locis … ingeniis.* Ablative absolute. Walsh (p. 194) points out that in this concluding phrase, Livy gives the reverse of the whole crossing, the theme of which has been the extreme *harshness* of places and dispositions of inhabitants.

49–51 *hoc maxime modo.* 'very much in this way/in the way I have described'. This phrase indicates the intention to be thorough and accurate but leaves open the possibility of inevitable uncertainties or inconsistencies, such as the fact that the crossing of the Alps took a few days longer than the fifteen he mentions (line 50 *quinto decimo die*).

50 *auctores.* These included Polybius (*c.*200–after 118 BC), a Greek historian who wrote about Rome's rise to power.

51 *Alpibus superatis.* There is a possible irony in that Hannibal conquered the Alps but ultimately failed to conquer Rome. Cf. the impact of Lucan's description of Caesar conquering the frozen Alps and contemplating the wars ahead (section 5.4 lines 1–3).

> ### Further reading
>
> - Walsh, P. G., *Livy Book XXI* (London: University Tutorial Press, 1975; rev. edn, London: Bristol Classical Press/Duckworth, 1985). Text, commentary and vocabulary.
> - De Sélincourt, A. (trans.) and Radice, B (ed.), *Livy: The War with Hannibal*, Penguin Classics, rev.repr. (Harmondsworth: Penguin, 1974).
> - Bradley, P., *Ancient Rome: Using Evidence* (Melbourne: Edward Arnold,1990; repr. Cambridge: Cambridge University Press, 2000). Detailed knowledge of the historical background is *not* required for the OCR GCSE in Latin, but this book is useful for reference or for students who wish to pursue questions on the Second Punic War and sources for it.

> ### Further teaching suggestions
>
> - What picture does Livy give of Hannibal as a leader?
> - How does Livy's account of the difficulties Hannibal met and the way he overcame them make him seem a worthy enemy of Rome?
> - In groups, students can find words used of the route and the troops' experiences that convey the hardships faced on the descent (lines 19–24, 25–31 and 32–39).
> - Read an extract from Polybius 3.54–56 and compare it with Livy's account of the descent.
> - Which parts of Livy's account do you find most interesting and why?

🌑 4. A traveller's tale—Horace *Satires* 1.5 (abridged)

As part of Maecenas' circle, Horace joined him at Anxur and accompanied him as far as Brundisium on a diplomatic mission to reconcile Octavian (the future emperor Augustus) and Mark Antony, in either 38 or 37 BC. In keeping with his insistence elsewhere (e.g. *Satires* 1.6) that his association with Maecenas, a prominent politician, did not give him inside information, he says little about the diplomacy and a great deal about the ups and downs of travel in good company. The earlier Roman satirist Lucilius also wrote a picaresque poem about a journey to Sicily, but it is likely that Horace drew together features of a particular journey with Maecenas and other companions and features of other journeys or travel in general as well as allusions to Lucilius.

Themes for exploration
- Style: mock epic, personification
- Health and travel
- Fellow travellers
- Discomfort

Metre—Hexameters

People and places

Aricia—a town at the foot of the Alban hills, on the Via Appia about 16 miles from Rome

Heliodorus—a teacher of rhetoric and one of Horace's companions on his journey

Forum Appi—modern Foro Appio, a small town about 27 miles from Aricia

(Via) Appia—road running south from Rome to Capua, named after the censor Appius Claudius Caecus, who had the road begun in 312 BC. It was later extended to Brundisium. For a detailed map see www.en.wikipedia.org/wki/Appian_Way.

Pomptine marshes—a low-lying marshy area that defeated attempts to drain it properly for centuries

Feronia—a local goddess who gave her name to a grove and fountain

Anxur—this town (modern Terracina) marked the southern end of the canal

Maecenas—Gaius Cilnius Maecenas, Horace's patron, but undertaking this journey in a diplomatic role

Cocceius—Lucius Cocceius Nerva, Maecenas' companion on his journey to Brundisium

Fonteius Capito—the third diplomat in the party

Marcus Antonius—83–30 BC, Roman statesman and general, rival of Octavian (the later emperor Augustus)

Marcus Plotius Tucca—friend of Virgil and Horace, one of Maecenas' circle

Lucius Varius Rufus—a friend of Virgil; he and Virgil introduced Horace to Maecenas.

Sinuessa—modern Bagnoli, on the coast

Virgil—Publius Vergilius Maro, the poet whose works included the epic *Aeneid*, and another member of Maecenas' literary circle

Caudium—a town on the Via Appia, between Beneventum and Capua; modern Montesarchio

Beneventum—modern Benevento

Apulia—modern Puglia, in south-eastern Italy, the region where Horace was born

Canusium—town in Apulia; modern Canosi, between Bari and Foggia

Rubi—modern Ruvo di Puglia, nearly 30 miles from Canusium

Barium—modern Bari, on the coast

Gnatia—also known as **Egnatia**, is modern Monopoli or Torre d'Agnazzio, on the coast

Brundisium—modern Brindisi; in Roman times a major port for travellers to Greece and the eastern provinces. It marked the end of the Via Appia.

Notes on text

Lines 1–9

These lines succinctly open up themes that recur in the rest of the poem.

1 *egressum* immediately establishes Horace's setting out from Rome, the first of many **departures**, described in different ways.

Aricia, Appia, **personification**.

2 *hospitio modico*, contrasting with *magna ... Roma*: the basic **accommodation** travellers experienced in the ancient world once they left home.

Heliodorus: good and distinguished **company** on the journey.

4 *differtum ... malignis*: **problematic transport**.

7–8 *hic... bellum*: **health problems**.

indico bellum: **down-to-earth matters** described in **grandiose language**.

Lines 10–24

This section contrasts mock epic grandeur with down-to-earth scenes on the canal journey over the Pomptine marshes, a malarial area just to the south east of Rome.

10–11 *iam nox ... signa parabat*. With Night personified, these lines have an epic tone that contrasts with Horace's upset stomach and missed dinner.

12–13 *tum ... ingerere. tum*, another epic touch, often introduces a momentous event, but here, instead of heroic warriors, we have the haggling of travellers' slaves and the boatmen. *ingerere* is a vivid historic infinitive, in keeping with the epic style, contrasting with the events.

15 *mali culices ranaeque palustres*. These would evoke the Pomptine marshes without Horace having to name them. *culices* are probably malarial mosquitoes. They and the frogs, as much as the people, are in contrast with the epic grandeur of the introductory lines 10–11.

21 *iamque dies aderat*. The day comes as majestically as the night, bringing not an epic battle but a fight between an impatient passenger and the boatman.

Lines 25–34

In these lines, congenial places and people are introduced, in contrast to the encounters of the previous section.

25 *Feronia*. A local goddess who gave her name to a place which is personified and provides long-awaited refreshment for the travellers. *lavimus*: an archaic equivalent of *lavamus*.

27 *impositum ... Anxur*. The town of Tarracina, built on an outcrop of white limestone.

28–33 *Maecenas ... Cocceius ... Capito*. With these names, the purpose of the journey emerges, the diplomatic meeting of Octavian (the future emperor Augustus) and Mark Antony, the 'friends who had fallen out' (30) whom in this case Maecenas, Cocceius and Fonteius Capito were to try to reconcile. They are all praised, Fonteius Capito being approved as a piece of smooth joinery, presenting no flaws or roughness to the discerning nail of the joiner.

Horace would have been there as part of the entourage of Maecenas, his patron; he modestly shows that he had no part in the diplomacy by choosing this point to mention his eye complaint.

Lines 35–46

The journey hits another high point as more literary figures arrive: Marcus Plotius Tucca and Lucius Varius Rufus (Virgil's executors who published the *Aeneid* after his death) and Virgil himself. After a few lines of praise for friendship, the narrative of the journey continues.

35 *postera ... gratissima*. Cf. the grandly described but disappointing dawn in line 21.

36 *Sinuessae*. At modern Bagnoli, on the coast.

40–41 *villula ... salemque*. The local officials were obliged to provide shelter and basic commodities to those travelling on official business.

43–44 *lusum ... crudis*. This is the closest the discreet Horace comes to revealing personal details about his famous companions: Maecenas playing ball, and he and Virgil suffering too much from travellers' ailments even to accompany Maecenas, apparently not the kind of patron who would make unreasonable demands on his ailing entourage.

45 *plenissima villa.* The grandeur of Cocceius' villa, described in the superlative, contrasts with the diminutive *villula* of line 40. It contrasts also with the humble inns (*cauponas*) which it is above in all senses of the word.

Lines 47–57

A series of hardships on the next stage of the journey. Students might notice that they all involve burning of different kinds: burnt dinner, a scorching wind and excessive smoke when leafy branches are burnt.

47 *recta* (*via*): ablative

Beneventum. Modern Benevento, 12 miles on from Cocceius' villa at Caudium. The travellers left the Via Appia at this point.

47–52 *ubi … videres.* Another mock epic scene, as the over-anxious host almost catches fire when dinner and house are threatened by flames. The personification of the fire as the god Vulcan, and the epic *tum … videres* (for *tum* see line 12)—'then you might see …'

53–55 *incipit … erepsemus.* Apulia was Horace's native region, as he was born in Venusia. He alludes to this in the word *notos* and in the local word *Atabulus* for the local scirocco or hot Saharan wind that affects southern Europe.

55–57 *nisi … camino.* Hospitality with a drawback in the form of smoke, painful for Horace's sore eyes no doubt: the transferred epithet *lacrimoso* emphasises the effect of the smoke on the people in whom it induces tears.

Lines 58–64

A section of more ups and downs for travellers, with a series of contrasts.

58 *rapimur.* Contrasts with the painful *erepsemus* of line 54.

59–60 *mansuri … perfacile est. est* means 'it is possible' here. Various places have been suggested for this town, but it was not uncommon for poets to have to get round referring to places that would not fit the metre (in line 37 of this *Satire*, not included in this selection, Formiae does not scan and is referred to as 'the city of the Mamurrae', one of its well-known families).

63 *Canusi.* The other half of this line ((*aquae non ditior urna*, omitted in the text in the Students' Book, but included on the audio CD) explains that Canusium is no better off for water either: Horace describes Apulia as 'thirsty' in *Epode* 3.16.

64 *Varius discedit.* Varius' departure causes him sadness and his friends weep, showing their mutual feelings and contrasting with the joy of the day when they all met (lines 35 ff.) There is perhaps also a contrast between the tears induced by smoke in line 56 and these which arise from genuine feeling.

Lines 65–72

Despite bad roads, the travellers reach the end of their journey, and the poet of his poem. An accumulation of place-names suggests a quickening pace as the end is in sight.

65–66 *inde … imbri.* Rubos. Rubi (modern Ruvo) is about 30 miles from Canusium, a longer journey and owing to rain and bad roads a slower one than the previous day, hence *fessi pervenimus.*

67–68 *postera … piscosi.* On a better day but with worse weather, they reach Barium (modern Bari). *piscosi* could imply a mixed blessing: they have at last reached the coast, but perhaps there was also the smell of fish in the air.

68–71 *dein Gnatia … cupit.* Gnatia or Egnatia (modern Monopoli or Torre d'Agnazzio) is mocked for laying claim to the spontaneous combustion of incense (*flamma sine*), the amusement heightened by the personification of the place and the grandiose way of saying there was no water there (the ablative absolute *Lymphis iratis*). A similar phenomenon at Egnatia is described by Pliny the Elder (*Natural History* 2.240), and Brown suggests the superstition arose from volcanic activity. Horace's scepticism reflects his Epicurean belief that the gods did not intervene in the lives of mortals. (Cf. the ode by Horace, section 6.6.).

72 *Brundisium … est. longae* goes with both *chartae* and *viae*, though the poem is concise. It was not the end of the journey for the diplomats who were making for either Athens or Tarentum, depending on which embassy the poem concerns. See above on lines 28–33, where Horace also distances himself from the diplomatic work of the VIPs he has been accompanying.

Further teaching suggestions

- 🔊 Listen to the recording on the audio CD (tracks 24–30) to get a sense of the metre and pace of the poem.
- To give an overview of the content and style, and to help students see beyond the separate episodes, use the notes on the first section as a checklist for recurring features in the rest of the poem. This might be kept as a table:

Content		Lines
	Departures	
	Accommodation	
	Company	
	Transport problems	
	Health problems	
Style		Lines
	Grandiose language	
	Personification	

- Collect words or phrases that describe the travel itself. Which ones convey fast travel and which slow?
- 🔊 Listen to the recording on the audio CD of sub-sections 2 (lines 10–24: track 25) and 5 (lines 47–57: track 28). How does the reading bring out the mock epic lines in these sections?
- If this were a modern journey:
  - (a) Students might imagine editing a holiday video of the journey, choosing three or four scenes to highlight.
  - (b) Which places would you be most likely to send postcards from, based on picturesqueness and/ or what happened there?

Further reading

- Brown, P. Michael, *Horace Satires I* (Oxford: Aris and Phillips, 1993). Translation and commentary.
- Fraenkel, E. *Horace* (Oxford: Oxford University Press, 1957; repr. 1980). Still a standard work.
- Rudd, N. (trans.), *The Satires of Horace and Persius*, Penguin Classics, rev. repr. (Harmondsworth: Penguin, 2005).
- Rudd, N., *The Satires of Horace* (Cambridge: Cambridge University Press, 1966; Bristol: Bristol Classical Press, 1982).
- Tennick, M., Handbook to *Libellus: Selections from Horace, Martial, Ovid and Catullus*, Cambridge Latin Texts (Cambridge: Cambridge University Press, 1978). Out of print. Commentary on first 33 lines.

⦿ 5. A storm at sea—Virgil *Aeneid* 1.81–123

A supernatural storm hits the Trojans as they sail from Sicily. Although initiated by the god of the winds, it is not only a gale but a storm, involving every element: clouds bring darkness and there is thunder and lightning.

Themes for exploration

- Storms as agents of the gods
- Fear of death at sea
- Pathos
- Style: descriptions and sound effects

Metre—Hexameters

People and places

Trojans (Teucri)—people of Troy, defeated by the Greeks in the Trojan War

Aeneas—Trojan prince, destined by the gods to sail for Italy and found a settlement there, leading eventually to the founding of Rome by his descendants

Troy—See above on Trojans

Tydides = Diomedes—a Greek hero

Aeacides = Achilles—a Greek hero

Hector—Trojan prince and hero

Sarpedon—a warrior from Lycia in Asia Minor who fought on the Trojan side

Simois—a river of Troy

Altars (Arae)—treacherous rocks off the North African coast

Syrtes—the name of two sandbanks off the North African coast

Lycians—See above on Sarpedon

Orontes, Ilioneus, Abas, Aletes—Trojan warriors

Achates—Trojan warrior and companion of Aeneas

Notes on text

Lines 1–11

The storm begins with a rush, indicated by forceful verbs at the beginning of the lines and rapid dactyls including repetitions of *–que*.

1–2 *haec … latus*. The subject of *impulit* is Aeolus, and the alliteration in the phrase *cavum conversa montem* draws attention to his fateful action.

2–6 *venti … fluctus*. The winds gather like an enemy force (*agmine*), and are strongly personified. It is a feature of storms in literature that they are caused by all the winds acting together. Cf. Homer *Odyssey* 5.295 f. Unlike Homer, Virgil does not mention the west wind, but adds detail to the African wind: 'full of tempests/hurricanes'. *procella* can also refer to a military onslaught or political upheaval, which may be relevant as Aeneas is heading for Carthage on the North African coast, the site of his own personal upheaval involving Dido (*Aeneid* 4), but also its later repercussions in the Punic Wars between Rome and Carthage (see passage 3 above), and, for Virgil, in the recent history of the conflict with Mark Antony and Cleopatra in Egypt (see section 6.7).

6 *et … fluctus*. The heavy spondees of the menacing waves contrast with the surrounding dactylic lines.

7–9 *insequitur … atra*. The storm's impact moves to the Trojans as darkness covers them.

10–11 *intonuere … mortem*. The thunder, in both poles, seems to surround them, and would seem to be a sign from the gods, over and above the danger of the storm itself.

Lines 12–21

Aeneas' terror and despair at the storm, a passage close to Odysseus' exclamation (Homer *Odyssey* 5.297 ff.)

12 *frigore.* The chill of terror as well as physical cold.

13 *duplices ... palmas.* The ancient posture of prayer.

14–21 *o terque ... volvit!* There are a number of strands in Aeneas' longing to have died on the battle field, incorporating emotive images from the Trojan War: even **dying before the eyes of his father**, normally considered tragic, would have been better than this; it would have been more honourable to meet **death at the hands of a hero** like Diomedes; the strength of his feeling is emphasised by the reference to the **death of Hector**, dragged around the walls of Troy by Achilles—even a shameful death like that would have been preferable; if a watery grave were decreed, his **native river Simois** would have been more hospitable than this stormy sea. See passage 2b lines 17–19 for a similar comparison between death at the hands of an enemy and death at sea, perhaps reflecting Rome's greater success as a power on land rather than sea.

Lines 22–32

The ways in which the storm disposes of the ships

22–25 *talia ... mons.* Even as Aeneas speaks, a fresh blast strikes the ship, leaving her broadside on to the waves (*dat latus*). *insequitur,* as in line 7, denotes the remorseless impact of the storm and its impact, here of the unstoppable mountainous wave. The final monosyllable and the three dactyls suggest the steepness of the wave or its breaking.

26–27 *hi ... harenis.* These lines contrast the lifting up of some sailors (*hi*), who seem to hang or dangle on the crest of the wave, with those to whom (*his*) the depth of the ocean is exposed with its seething sand.

28–32 *tres ... harenae.* In lines 28 and 30, the magical *tres ... tres ...* (cf. *ter,* line 36) underlines the supernatural working of the storm: three ships are driven onto rocks, one common seafaring hazard, three face another, as they are stranded on sandbanks, quickly driven from deep to shallow water. These sandbanks off the African coast, the Syrtes, were a constant danger for ancient seafarers: cf. the Acts of the Apostles (famous for its description of journeys by sea made by Saint Paul), chapter 28 verse 17.

Lines 33–43

This section describes the pathos of the sailors overwhelmed by the storm: a helmsman thrown overboard; his ship caught in a whirlpool; scattered sailors swimming; the remnants of Trojan treasures spread over the waves. The pathos is ironic, as we know that the men will be saved, the storm halted by Neptune. As in lines 1–11, the action is conveyed in verbs at the beginning of lines 36–38 and 42–43.

35–36 *in puppim ... caput.* The force of the water is emphasised by the combination of a strong break at *ferit* and the following dactyls.

37–38 *torquet ... vasto.* More dactyls, conveying the whirlpool, contrast with the laboured movement of the sailors in the following line.

40–43 *iam ... fatiscunt.* The repetition of *iam* and *qua* emphasises the accumulation of defeats: the storm ends as it began, described as an enemy (*vicit, inimicum imbrem*).

Further teaching suggestions

Content

- 🔊 Listen to the recording on the audio CD (tracks 31–34) to get the shape of the four passages: the violent onset of the storm, followed by the different tone of Aeneas' words, then the violent destructiveness of the storm and finally the pathos of the shipwrecks and the victory of the storm.
- Compare the storm in Homer *Odyssey* 5.291–318.
- How do Aeneas' words in lines 12–21 contribute to the content?

Style

- 🔊 Listen to the audio CD (tracks 31–34), first to get a general impression of the metre, and then to focus on lines with particularly striking effects, e.g. lines 1, 4–9, 25, 36–38 and 42–43 mentioned in the notes above.
- Explore the effect of the use of proper nouns (winds, places and people).
- Compare these translations of the second half of line 25:
  - (a) On came, towering, a piled precipice of water. (Knight)
  - (b) … and then, piled up there, a precipice of sea hung. (Day Lewis)

Further reading

- Page, T. E., *The Aeneid of Virgil Books I–VI* (London, Macmillan, 1962).
- Williams, R. D. (ed.), *The Aeneid of Virgil* (London: Macmillian, 1972–3; repr. London: Bristol Classical Press, 1996). Latin text, English introduction and notes.
- Gould, H. E. and Whiteley, J. L. (eds.), *Virgil: Aeneid 1* (Bristol: Bristol Classical Press, 1984; repr. London: Duckworth, 1991). Latin text, English introduction and notes; includes vocabulary.
- Day Lewis, C. (trans.), *Virgil: The Aeneid*. Oxford World's Classics (Oxford, Oxford University Press, 1952; repr. with notes and introduction by J. Griffin, 1986).
- Knight, W. F. Jackson (trans.), *Virgil: The Aeneid*, Penguin Classics (Harmondworth: Penguin, 1956; rev. repr. 1973).
- West, D. A. (trans.), *Virgil, The Aeneid: A new prose translation* (London: Penguin, 2001).

6. The ship of state in troubled waters—Horace *Odes* 1.14

This poem has been read as a straightforward description of a ship in trouble. However, the sustained personification of the ship and the impassioned description of the ship as *desiderium curaque non levis* (lines 17–18) suggest something more. There are also parallels with fragments by the Greek lyric poet Alcaeus (the metre of Horace's poem is Alcaic), which explicitly concern the state. Furthemore, the language of steering a ship was a commonplace in talking about government; for instance Cicero anticipates his own departure from government in terms of leaving the ship and witnessing shipwrecks from the land (Cicero *Letters to Atticus* 2.7.4). What particular crisis the poem reflects is not known, but it could date from or at least refer to the unsettled period of hostility between Octavian and Antony some years before the battle of Actium in 31 BC (see section 6.7). West (pp. 146–7) suggests it could have been written later and have a particular relevance to Augustus at a time when he might have been in danger. In fact the allegory enables Horace to talk about the state without mentioning any specific and therefore sensitive events and the involvement of individuals.

Themes for exploration

- A ship at the mercy of the sea
- A ship as a metaphor of the state

Metre—Fourth Asclepiad

People and places

Cyclades—islands around the island of Delos, in the Aegean Sea

Notes on text

Lines 1–10

If these lines are taken as an allegory of the state in trouble, it is not for that reason necessary that every detail of the description should correspond precisely to an aspect of the state, beyond a general equation of waves with unrest, the harbour with peace and the battered ship with the state itself.

2–9 *o quid agis ... aequor?* The ship's plight is described in urgent personal address to the ship.

5 *Africo.* The stormy southwest wind, but in a political context the term could also invoke the stormy relations between Rome and Africa (see note above on 5.2–6).

10 *non di.* Possibly a reflection of Horace's avowed agnosticism in his poetry (cf. section 6.6), but a desperate appeal to gods who seem absent is a natural reaction. Cf. 5.13 ff.

11–16 *quamvis ... cave.* The personification continues, becoming more distinctly female, the adjective *Pontica* increasing her pedigree as 'a daughter of a famous forest'. The ship is warned not to put trust in her appearance any more than her ancestry and name. *ludibrium* conveys a ship tossed at the mercy of the winds, but the word is also used where violence is done to a woman.

17–18 *nuper ... levis.* The contrast seems to be between the anxiety of earlier unrest, perhaps when Horace felt out of sympathy with the prevailing politics (Michie suggests a connection with his fighting on the Republican side in his younger days), and the current regime, which he loves and is anxious for. West suggests that the word *desiderium* could imply that Augustus is away from Rome; the same word is used in *Odes* 4.5.15 in connection with Augustus' long absence from Rome in 16–13 BC.

20 *vites ... Cycladas.* The subjunctive *vites* has an imperative force. As with *Pontica* (line 11), *Cycladas* adds geographical detail and vividness.

Further teaching suggestions

Content

- 🔊 Listen to the audio CD (track 35). Which moods of the poem does the reading bring out?
- Which aspects of the personification of the boat do you find most effective?
- Is there a contemporary situation that could be treated allegorically as a journey on a stormy sea?

Style

- 🔊 Listen to the audio CD (track 35) to get a sense of the metre, and the way in which the meaning cuts across the ends of lines.
- List the adjectives Horace uses. How do they show the vulnerability of the ship?

Further reading

- Quinn. K., *Horace: Odes* (London: Macmillan Educational, 1980; London: Bristol Classical Press/Duckworth, 1996).
- Michie, J. (trans.), *The Odes of Horace*, Penguin Classics (Harmondworth: Penguin, 1964). Verse translation, preserving some of the original metres, and notes. Out of print.
- West, D. (trans.), *Horace: The Complete Odes and Epodes*, Oxford World's Classics (Oxford: Oxford University Press, 1997). A more literal translation than Michie's, with notes and biographical information
- Fraenkel, E., *Horace* (Oxford: Oxford University Press, 1957; repr. 1980). Still a standard work.

5 CONFLICT AND CONQUEST

Content overview

Prose

1. Bravery and strategy in battle: Caesar *Gallic War*
2. Caesar at the heart of battle against the Belgae: Caesar *Gallic War*
3. Inspiration for the fight: Tacitus *Annals*
4. Marital conflict: Cicero *Ad Atticum*

🔊 **Verse**

5. Atalanta meets her match: Ovid *Metamorphoses*
6. Advice for would-be lovers: Ovid *Ars Amatoria*

Themes in this section

Conflict	1, 2, 3, 4, 5, 6
in war	1, 2, 3
in love	4, 5
Leadership	1, 2, 3, 6
Personal conflict between individuals	1, 4, 5
Conquest	1, 3, 5, 6
Powerful women	3, 5

1. Bravery and strategy in battle—Caesar *Gallic War* 5.44–48 (abridged)

After his expedition to Britain, Caesar has returned to Gaul amidst trouble from the Gallic tribes. The Roman forces are all settled in their various separate winter quarters, late in 54 BC, when there is a large-scale revolt by the Gauls. Caesar himself is, at the time of these extracts, at Samarobriva (Amiens), 100 miles to the west of Cicero.

Themes for exploration

- Bravery and leadership in battle
- Personal conflict between individuals
- Caesar's language in constructing a dramatic picture of battle
- The characters of Pullo, Vorenus and Vertico

People and places

Titus Pullo—centurion of the Eleventh Legion, who later serves under Mark Antony before encouraging his men to change sides and serve under Pompey during the Civil War

Lucius Vorenus—centurion of the Eleventh Legion. Both he and Pullo feature in the BBC series *Rome* (see Further reading below)

Nervius—the Nervii were one of the Belgic tribes inhabiting the area of northeastern France and Belgium

Vertico—one of the Nervii

Gallus—Gallic or a Gaul

Cicero—Quintus Tullius Cicero, the younger brother of Cicero the orator, in command of a legion in the territory of the Nervii, possibly at Binche on the River Sambre

Notes on text

Lines 1–25

Caesar's abundantly clear style immediately sets out the facts that Pullo and Vorenus are leading centurions vying for top spot (**1–2**). He records the sparky challenge of Pullo in direct speech with two questions (**5–6**). Pullo follows his words with action—*procedit* (**7**) is prominently positioned and *irrumpit* (**8**) is a rather forceful verb. Vorenus quite naturally has to react, fearing what others will think of him (**9–10**). With one javelin throw, Pullo is in the thick of the action and the enemy turn on him (**10–13**). So graphic is the detail with regard to Pullo's battle equipment (**14–15**), we realise that at some point an eye-witness must have reported the details to Caesar. Pullo is quickly surrounded, and Vorenus comes to his aid. The focus of the narrative, like the focus of the enemy, necessarily shifts to Vorenus with *ad hunc* (**17**). Vorenus drives the enemy back (**18–20**), but then he too finds himself in a difficult position (**20–21**). Pullo comes to his assistance (**21**) and they both return victorious to the camp after fighting their way out of trouble (**21–23**). The balanced phrasing of *in contentione et certamine* (**23**), and *alter alteri/uter utri* (**24/25**) emphasises Caesar's almost moralistic tale that the top spot between these two brave centurions cannot be discerned.

Lines 26–36

The expression *in dies* combined with two comparative adjectives, and a superlative adverb (**26**), in addition to the *quanto … tanto …* structure (**26–28**), all add to the idea that Caesar has much to deal with and that the situation is difficult. Particularly graphic is what happens to some of the messengers who are caught by the enemy (crucifixion: **30**). The short character sketch of Vertico (**31–32**) gives some idea of the tactics Cicero needs to employ. In part of the text not included here, we learn that Caesar receives this letter from Cicero via Vertico at about 5 pm. Overnight he summons help from Crassus, Gaius Fabius, and Labienus, who command other legions in other areas. Labienus is unable to help, but Crassus' forces join with Caesar and the following morning they set out. Caesar has a much smaller force (about 7,000 men) than he had planned.

Lines 37–51

Having made long marches (**37**), Caesar's ingenuity is once again to the fore in the advice which he gives a messenger (**40–45**). The fact that the smoke from fires (**50**) quickly follows Cicero's reading of the letter shows that all is well and that Caesar is on his way. We learn in the continuation of this passage, not reproduced here, that the Gauls then abandon their siege of Cicero's camp, and after going to meet Caesar, are routed.

Further teaching suggestions

- Construct a storyboard for a film script of battle scene involving Pullo and Vorenus.
- Collect Latin examples of how the whole tale is made vivid.
- Discuss what makes for good leadership/ bravery in war, and collect responses as to how Caesar, Cicero, Pullo and Vorenus all match up to these ideals.

Further reading

- Caesar, *Gallic War V*, ed. R. C. Carrington (London: Duckworth, 1991).
- Translations of the works of Caesar (widely available).
- The BBC TV Series *Rome* for further fictional depiction of Pullo and Vorenus (although not historically accurate, and possibly with a certificate preventing some GCSE students watching the DVD).
- Goldsworthy, Adrian, *Caesar: The Life of a Colossus* (London: Weidenfeld & Nicolson, 2006).
- Goldsworthy, Adrian, *The Complete Roman Army* (London: Thames & Hudson, 2003).
- Cowan, Ross, *Roman Battle Tactics 109BC– AD313* (Oxford: Osprey, 2007).
- Gilliver, Catherine, *Caesar's Gallic Wars 58–51 BC*, Essential Histories 43 (Oxford: Osprey, 2002).

2. Caesar at the heart of the battle against the Belgae—Caesar *Gallic War* 2.20

Themes for exploration

- Caesar, the all-action hero
- The language Caesar uses to describe his own actions
- A vivid battle scene
- Leadership and the qualities demanded of both a leader and an ordinary soldier

Notes on text

This passage was chosen to show Caesar at the very centre of battle. There are no other proper nouns to be explained. That in itself is significant. The need for his action is expressed through the various gerundives of obligation (**1–5**). Their quick succession, together with the occasional *oportet* (**2**) or part thereof, illustrate the first clause admirably. The switch to abstract nouns in the second part of the text (**6–14**) allows the focus to fall, quite rightly upon the actions of Caesar's men—they naturally respond to his leadership and the demands placed upon them by the situation (**7–14**). His training of them and his leadership is evident throughout.

Further teaching suggestions

- Focus on the list of activities which demonstrate Caesar's multi-tasking.

Further reading

- Kennedy, E. (ed.), *Caesar: Gallic War II* (London: Duckworth, 2008).
- Translations of the works of Caesar (widely available).
- The BBC TV Series *Rome* for further fictional depiction of Pullo and Vorenus, (although not historically accurate, and possibly with a certificate preventing some GCSE students watching the DVD).
- Goldsworthy, Adrian, *Caesar: The Life of a Colossus* (London: Weidenfeld & Nicolson, 2006).
- Goldsworthy, Adrian, *The Complete Roman Army* (London: Thames & Hudson, 2003).
- Cowan, Ross, *Roman Battle Tactics 109BC–AD313* (Oxford: Osprey, 2007).
- Gilliver, Catherine, *Caesar's Gallic Wars 58–51 BC*, Essential Histories 43 (Oxford: Osprey, 2002).

3. Inspiration for the fight—Tacitus *Annals* 14.35–37

These passages provide the student with fascinating accounts from Roman Britain, allowing not only character sketches but also a glimpse into Roman warfare, and a sight of the Britons from a Roman point of view.

Themes for exploration

- The Romans in Britain
- Tacitus' character sketches of Boudicca and Suetonius
- The reasons and motivations for conflict
- The concept of a just war
- The leadership and rhetoric required in such a situation
- A woman in a military role
- The vivid description of a battle scene

People and places

Boudicca—queen of the tribe of the Iceni (from East Anglia), wife of King Prasutagus, b. AD 4. She had been flogged and her daughters raped by the Romans.

Suetonius—Gaius Suetonius Paulinus, governor of Britain from AD 59. His first two years were successful, but then following an attack on Anglesey, the Iceni tribe revolted in the southern part of East Anglia. This battle is thought to have taken place somewhere in the West Midlands. It is known both as the Battle of Watling Street and the Battle of Paulerspury.

Poenius Postumus—camp prefect of the Second Legion (*Legio Secunda Augusta*). He neglected to heed the call of Suetonius to join forces against the revolt of the Iceni.

Notes on text

Lines 1–13

Tacitus' brevity enhances the urgency of the situation for Boudicca. The simplicity of presenting her daughters (part of her reason for fighting) to each tribe adds to Boudicca's reasoning about the leadership of women for the Britons. The indirect speech begins here with *testabatur* (**3**). Tacitus then has Boudicca emphasise her own claim to authority as one which is not based on her role as queen and on her wealth (*sed tunc non ut ...* : **3**), but through the mistreatment which she has suffered

(highlighted by the tricolon of tragic things which have happened to her—*libertatem amissam, confectum ... corpus, contrectatam filiarum pudicitiam*: **4–5**). She remarks that Roman lust and pillage have gone so far as to leave neither bodies, nor old age, nor virginity untouched, and claims that she has the gods on her side (**5–8**). She encourages the Britons by pointing out the weaknesses of the Romans' situation (*cecidisse ... circumspicere*: **8–9**). Her negatives (*ne ... quidem, nedum*: **9, 10**) suggest what the Romans will not tolerate, and she concludes with the stark ultimatum of conquer or fall (*vincendum ... vel cadendum esse*: **11–12**). Her final statement about the resolve of women is equally emphatic (**12–13**).

Lines 14–26

The correct, and almost formal, terms used of Suetonius' speech (*exhortationes et preces*: **15**) are contrasted with Tacitus' description of the barbarians' noises (*sonores barbarorum et inanes minas*: **16**). The indirect speech begins at *plus illic ...* (**16**) and there is a neat employment of similar language and content to that used by Boudicca with the immediate contrast that the Romans are looking more at women than strapping young men (**17**). This is followed by a belittling of the barbarians' readiness for war (*imbelles, inermes*: **17**), and a statement of how they will fall apart against that classic Roman combination of *ferrum virtutemque* (**18**). The inspiration for collective victory is provided through an appeal to individual skill and desire for glory to be one of the few upon whom the rest have relied (**19–21**). The final part of Suetonius' address gives practical advice both for the fight and for ensuring a sensible victory. They must be oblivious to plunder (*praedae immemores*: **23**), and that way everything will fall under their sway (*cuncta ipsis cessura*: **23**). The effect is immediate and the soldiers ready themselves for war.

Lines 27–41

The Roman forces hold their position (*gradu immota et angustias … retinens*: **27–28**) and then move out in a wedge formation (**29**). The cavalry with spears extended deal with those areas of strong resistance which are offered (*eques protentis hastis …*: **29–30**). The enemy find flight difficult (*difficili effugio*: **31**), and the slaughter includes women and beasts of burden (**32–33**). Tacitus' use of numbers to sum up the situation is very effective (**35–36**). So too is the short sentence telling of the end of Boudicca (**37**). Poenius Postumus cannot face the shame (**37–41**).

> ### Further teaching suggestions
>
> - Construct a bullet-point table summarising the speeches of both Boudicca and Suetonius Paulinus.
> - Ask students to write and reconstruct a speech inspiring their troops before such a battle—either as Boudicca or Suetonius Paulinus using the main points from the table.

> ### Further reading
>
> - Woodcock, E. C. (ed.), *Tacitus: Annals XIV*, Latin Texts (London: Bristol Classical Press, 1992; repr. of Methuen's Classsical Text edn 1939).
> - Miller, Norma, *Tacitus Annals XIV: A Companion Book to Book 14 of Tacitus: The Annals of Imperial Rome …* , Classical Studies (London: Bristol Classical Press, 1987).
> - Translations of Tacitus' *Annals* (widely available).
> - Hill, S. and Ireland, S., *Roman Britain*, Classical World (London: Bristol Classical Press, 1998).
> - Goldsworthy, Adrian, *The Complete Roman Army* (London: Thames & Hudson, 2003).
> - Cowan, Ross, *Roman Battle Tactics 109BC–AD313* (Oxford: Osprey, 2007).

4. Marital conflict—Cicero *Ad Atticum* 1.5.2 and 5.1.23–24

These extracts from letters from Cicero to his close friend, Atticus, tell of the marital conflict between Cicero's brother and his wife (Atticus' sister). The first extract is from the early years of the marriage, whilst the second is from 51 BC. They are moving between their villa at Arpinum and property at Aquinum when this incident occurs.

Themes for exploration

- Conflict within marriage
- The involvement of relatives
- The personal nature of Cicero's letters to Atticus
- The detailed recall of incidents from the perspective of one side of an argument.

People and places

Atticus—Titus Pomponius Atticus, Cicero's closest friend and correspondent. He was of the equestrian order and was a banker and editor. He and Cicero were educated together, and he gains the name 'Atticus' from his love for the city of Athens, where he stayed for part of his education.

Quintus—Quintus Tullius Cicero, Cicero's younger brother (b. 102 BC, d. 43 BC), a soldier and administrator, married to Pomponia in 69 BC

Pomponia—wife of Quintus, (and mother of their child of the same name), and sister of Atticus. The couple divorced in 45/44 BC

Arpinum—a town in Latium, the birthplace of Cicero

Arcanum—in Latium, where Quintus has a farm

Aquinum—a town in Latium

Notes on text

Lines 1–6

Here Cicero is anxious to point out how he tries to keep his brother in check in his relationship towards his wife, Pomponia, by means of letters. He remarks that he has tried to ensure that his brother's attitude to Pomponia is as it should be (*is qui esse deberet*: **2–3**), and goes on to tell Atticus that the nature of his advice has been threefold towards one who is his brother, is younger and is in the wrong (**4–5**). The three imperfect subjunctives in the first person reveal that threefold advice. His hope for the future of their marriage is stressed in the final words of the extract—he has received letters from which he trusts that all is both as it should be and as they would wish (*et oporteat et velimus*: **6**).

Lines 1–16

Cicero writes in a very personal fashion showing the closeness of his relationship to Atticus. He stresses the proper behaviour of Quintus towards Pomponia using both the superlative adverb *humanissime* (**2**) and the *cum … tum …* arrangement (**4**) to illustrate that as far as he can see, every aspect of Quintus' behaviour is correct. The reporting of the very words used by both Quintus (**2–3**) and Pomponia (**5–6**) shed a fascinating light upon the breakdown of a relationship: clearly we cannot know, as Cicero does not, some of the background to the quarrel. Pomponia's reply to Quintus is stark through its simple structure. Cicero tries to suggest a reason for this to Atticus, but he cannot read Pomponia's mind (**6–7**). The non-sequitur nature of the exchange highlights the conflict, as Quintus remarks upon his daily suffering (**7–8**). There is alliteration and balanced phrasing in his description of her response—*absurde et aspere verbis vultuque* (**9**). We might almost say 'roughly and rudely' or something similar. The short clauses when Quintus sends Pomponia something from the table (**10–11**) reflect the fractious interchange. Cicero's neat arrangement with *nihil* and two comparative adjectives (**11–12**) perhaps suggests he is trying to be even-handed and steer clear of trouble. We then hear of further developments after Cicero has departed (**12–16**).

<table>
<tr><td>

Further teaching suggestions

Obviously any discussion here needs to be sensitively handled.

- Ask students to collect Latin examples of Cicero's personal comments on the relationship of his brother and sister-in-law.

</td><td>

Further reading

- Translations of Cicero's letters (widely available).
- Everitt, Anthony, *Cicero: A Turbulent Life* (London: John Murray, 2001); published in the United States as *Cicero: The Life and Times of Rome's Greatest Politician* (New York: Random Press, 2001).
- Harris, Robert, *Imperium* (London: Hutchinson, 2006).

</td></tr>
</table>

5. Atalanta meets her match—Ovid *Metamorphoses* 10.560–680 (abridged)

Telling the story of Atalanta and Hippomenes through Venus' conversation with Adonis during their love-making allows Ovid to show off his superb narrative technique. Not only that, but his story within a story will also reveal another metamorphosis just after these extracts. Here it is through conflict, in the form of the race, that Hippomenes ultimately makes his conquest.

Themes for exploration

- Sport in the ancient world
- The role of women in the ancient world
- Conflict and conquest
- Requited/unrequited love
- The role of the gods (in epic)
- The idea of winning at all costs
- The drama of the situation
- The characters of Atalanta and Hippomenes

Metre—Hexameters

People and places

Venus—goddess of love and sex, telling this story to Adonis within the *Metamorphoses*

Adonis—a youth renowned for his beauty with whom Venus had an affair

Atalanta—daughter of Schoeneus, famous not only for her speed but also as a huntress. She was the first to hit the Calydonian boar, and as a result was loved by Meleager, who soon afterwards died.

Hippomenes—Atalanta's suitor, otherwise known as Melanion. He and Atalanta are subsequently turned into lions for either not

giving proper honour to Venus or for making love in a temple.

Neptunius—descended from Neptune—Hippomenes' grandfather or great-grandfather was Neptune via Onchestus, or Megareus and Onchestus.

Cytherea—Cythera is an island to the south of the Peloponnese in Greece. It was thought to be an island of Venus, and so she is referred to here as Cytherean.

Tamasenum—according to Ovid, a place in Cyprus

Cypria—of Cyprus, another island sacred to Venus

Megareius—an adjective used to describe Hippomenes, who is variously described as the son of Megareus, or Onchestus, who was also known as Megareus.

Schoeneia—describing Atalanta, daughter of Schoeneus

Notes on text

Lines 1–28

Venus begins in conversational fashion confirming rumour as fact by means of what is almost an aside (*superabat enim*: **3**). Her direct address to Adonis (*nec dicere posses*: **3**) gives us the knowledge that Atalanta was as beautiful as she was fast (**4**). The first part of the oracle tells Atalanta what she wants to hear (**5–6**), but the second half is not to her liking (**7**)—indeed she will not manage to flee or outrun a husband. The challenge she sets for would-be suitors is grand and dramatic: **10–13**. Her strong opening statement sets her up to be beaten and the position at the beginning of lines **12** and **13** of the contrast between rewards for the quick (*praemia veloci*) and death as the price for those who are slow (*mors pretium tardis*) adds to her harsh tone. The clipped nature of her final clause in line **13**, and the brief statement from Venus in line **14**, which is immediately followed by *sed*, allow our picture of Atalanta to continue in similar vein.

An air of gentle humour is emphasised by the initial incredulity of Hippomenes (**16–17**) together with Venus' aside to Adonis about their beauty in line **20**. The dramatic value of *obstipuit tollensque manus* (**21**) paints a very vivid picture, especially after Hippomenes' request for forgiveness (**21–23**). With his question to himself (**25–26**), we know he will race against Atalanta.

Lines 29–36

He sees the losing men from the previous race receive their punishment (**31**). Nevertheless both his physical presence in the middle (*constitit in medio*: **33**) and his fixed gaze (*vultuque in virgine fixo*: **33**) confirm his resolve in our eyes. His question is direct and addressed to Atalanta (*quaeris*: **34**), whilst his challenge is brief (*mecum confer*: **35**). He then begins telling Atalanta why it would be no shame to lose (**36**).

Lines 37–59

The *p* alliteration in the opening line of this extract may represent the repeated demands of both Atalanta's father and the crowd. Hippomenes' prayer is a brief one (**39–40**), and Venus tells Adonis of her benevolence, and her speed in assisting the young man (**42**). However her description of the field and the tree allows a dramatic build-up to the delivery of the three apples (**43–50**). The *fulva/fulvo* (**47**) repetition allows the tree to sound particularly special. After Venus' direct intervention, the race begins and various imagery assists in painting a picture of the speed of both runners (whether over the sea with dry feet (**53**) or over the tops of corn without damage (**54**)). The internal rhyme of *clamorque favorque* (**55**), combined with the anaphora of *nunc* (**56–57**), allow us to imagine the repeated noise and cheers of the spectators. The three imperatives make these shouts particularly dramatic (*propera/utere/pelle*), but Ovid keeps us guessing as to who will win in the final two lines of this passage.

Lines 60–78

The interjection *o quotiens* (**60**) allows us to follow the changing fortunes and emotions of both the competitors, and Hippomenes' first apple plays its part (**63–66**). Almost in the manner of a camera zooming and distancing, Ovid has us follow the apple as it rolls and stuns Atalanta. The brevity of *praeterit Hippomenes* (**67**) means that we focus on the young man's progress and the resultant applause. Atalanta is soon quite literally back on track. The second apple has only a brief effect (**70–71**), ensuring that the dramatic intervention of the third apple does far more, accompanied as it is by a brief prayer to Venus (**72**). The longer Ovid's description, the more we are necessarily allowed to view the events in slow motion. Venus cannot resist boasting to Adonis with verbs in the first person singular of all that she did (*coegi/adieci/inpediique*: **75–77**), and with almost smug wordplay (**78**), she brings her story of the race itself to an end announcing Hippomenes as the victor (**79**).

🔊 6. Advice for would-be lovers—Ovid *Ars Amatoria* 1.44–126 (abridged)

The *Ars Amatoria* is full of advice for would-be lovers on how to find a girlfriend or boyfriend. This extract presents students with some of Ovid's ideas, but also the idea that not all runs smoothly.

Themes for exploration

- Imagery of the natural world
- The search for love
- Attitudes to love
- Romulus and the Sabine women, the stories of early Rome
- Ancient theatre
- Ovid's humour, exaggeration and subtlety

Metre—Elegiacs

People and places

Andromeda—daughter of King Cepheus and his queen, Cassiopeia, whom Perseus rescued from a sea-monster. She had had to be given as food for the monster on account of Cassiopeia's boasts that she was more beautiful than the Nereids. As a result Neptune/Poseidon was angry. Perseus subsequently marries her.

Perseus—mythological Greek hero, and son of Jupiter/Zeus and Danae, who rescues Andromeda (from Ethiopia according to some, although Ovid records India here—referring in any case to a far-off place) after slaying Medusa

Phrygius—Phrygian, but here Trojan, referring to the stealing of Helen by Paris, so beginning the Trojan War

Graius—Greek. Here *Graia* refers to Helen.

Gargara—a city of the Troad, renowned for its fertility

Methymna—a town on the island of Lesbos

Aeneas—a prince of Troy, and founder of the line of those who founded Rome. Son of Anchises and Venus, goddess of love, and therefore the *mater* referred to here is Venus. The city referred to is Rome.

Romulus—traditional founder and first king of Rome

Sabinus—the Sabine hills are those hills to the north-east/east of Rome; the Sabines were in effect, Rome's neighbours.

Other references are explained in the Students' Book.

Notes on text

Lines 1–20

The hunting imagery is very prevalent at the beginning of this extract. Lovers must be like hunters or fishermen whatever their prey, and over the first five lines we see a variety of methods: so too will Ovid tell the lover where to look. His tone in line **6** is very direct and this is followed by an imperative *disce* (**7**). The next instruction is that he who is seeking love need not journey far (**9**) like Perseus had to, in order to bring Andromeda from India (**10**), or as Paris taking Helen (**11**). The *t* alliteration in line **12** may reflect the abundance of girls present in Rome. There are as many girls as Gargara has ears of corn, as Methymna has clusters of grapes (**14**), or getting back to the nature imagery which we saw at the beginning of this extract, as many as the fish in the sea, the birds in the air or the stars in the sky (**15–16**). Whatever age of girl takes a would-be lover's fancy (**18–19**), she will be found in Rome.

Lines 21–25

Ovid suggests one place in particular may be a successful one for lovers. *venare* (**21**) picks up the language of hunting, and in the lines which follow, students' attention should be drawn to the four options which Ovid presents to the lover reflecting the sheer multiplicity of love available. The nature simile involving ants and bees is vivid (**25–30**), and we may discuss how appropriate these are. The chiastic word arrangement in line **31** (*spectatum veniunt, veniunt spectentur*) reinforces Ovid's idea that there will inevitably be a loss of chastity in the theatre. Line **33** brings a wholly different image, but still one based on the theatre, this time as the venue for the rape of the Sabine women as organised by Romulus (**34–35**). Ovid uses various means to describe the theatre as particularly rough and rustic to create an air of antiquity, such that even the applause is not as sophisticated as 'modern' applause (**45**). Line **46** marks the signal from Romulus to his men for drama of a very different kind, and the attention of students should be drawn to the various nature similes which appear once more (**49–50**). The brief pictures of the Sabine women in varying states of distress will also merit discussion (**51–56**).

Further teaching suggestions

- Ask students to list the comparisons which Ovid makes with the natural world. How appropriate is each of these images for his advice to a lover?

- Have students construct an advice page from a modern celebrity magazine: it should contain Ovid's reply to an anxious lovelorn reader, as well as celebrity gossip examples based on Perseus and Andromeda, and Paris and Helen.

Further reading

- Translations of Ovid's love poetry (widely available).

- Lively, Genevieve, *Ovid Love Songs* (London: Duckworth, 2005).

- Armstrong, Rebecca, *Ovid and His Love Poetry* (London: Duckworth, 2005).

- Hardie, Philip (ed.), *The Cambridge Companion to Ovid* (Cambridge: Cambridge University Press, 2002).

6 PROPHECIES AND PORTENTS

Contents overview

1–3 Prose

1. Do you believe in ghosts?: Pliny *Letters*
2. The mysterious death of Romulus: Livy
   A History of Rome
3. Omens, portents and the murder of Julius
   Caesar: Suetonius *Divine Julius*

🔊 4–7 Verse

4. Caesar crosses the Rubicon: Lucan *Civil War*
5. Praying for profit: Persius *Satires*
6. A sign from heaven: Horace *Odes*
7. The shield of Aeneas: Virgil *Aeneid*

Themes in this section

Stories and incidents where the supernatural is prominent:	
ghosts	1
prophecies	4, 7
omens and portents	1, 3
deification	2, 3
visions	1, 2, 4
sense of numinous	6
rituals	3, 5
Description of supernatural events and the effect they have:	
figures of supernatural size	1, 4
light and darkness	1, 4, 6
awe	6, 7
fear	1
The role of the supernatural in Roman history and propaganda	2, 3, 7
Manipulation of the events or scepticism	1, 2, 3, 5, 7

1. Do you believe in ghosts?—Pliny *Letters* 7.27

This letter probably dates from the period (after AD 106) when Pliny had relinquished his responsibility for the River Tiber and when Licinius Sura had returned from the first Dacian War where he served on the emperor Trajan's staff. This accounts for the leisure Pliny claims both men now have. Pliny's three stories, the number necessary for scholarly debate, are presented as a variety of evidence on which Licinius Sura can make up his mind.

Themes for exploration

- Belief in the supernatural
- Story-telling: content and style
- Prophecies and careers

People and places

Quintus Curtius Rufus—a man from an obscure family, thought by some to be the son of a gladiator. He advanced as a politician through the support of the emperor Tiberius.

Carthage—a city on the north coast of Africa, traditionally believed to have been founded by Dido, and an enemy of Rome: the two Punic Wars were fought between 264 and 146 BC, when Rome finally defeated Carthage.

Athens—major city of Greece

Athenodorus—either Athendorus of Tarsus, friend of the emperor Augustus and teacher, or an unknown person

Domitian—emperor AD 81–96. In the later years of his reign, fearing plots against him, he instituted a 'reign of terror' dependent on informers.

Notes on text

Lines 1–15

Pliny begins in a spirit of scientific enquiry but quickly moves to the first of his stories.

2–5 *esse phantasmata ... accipere.* Lucretius and the Greek philosopher Democritus among others believed that dreams and visions had a material existence (*propriam figuram numenque*), whereas Aristotle explained them psychologically as the consequence of an individual's state of mind (*ex metu nostro imaginem accipere*).

6 *Curtio Rufo.* Quintus Curtius Rufus, possibly the historian of Alexander the Great. His career developed, partly with the support of Tiberius, as he became praetor and then consular legate of Lower Germany in about AD 47. When he was consul or when he went to Africa as proconsul is not known. Tacitus also tells this story, which he sets in Hadrumetum in Africa (*Annals* 11.21).

7 *inclinato die.* The early afternoon may seem a surprising time for a ghost to appear but it is a quiet time of day in hot countries where people retreat indoors and take a siesta.

8 *mulieris ... pulchriorque.* For a similar embodied personification see passage 6.4 where Rome appears to Caesar as a woman. Africa also appears on Roman coinage as a woman.

9–11 *Africam ... moriturum.* The omission of the parts of the auxiliary *esse* makes the prophecy more concise and direct. After *gesturum* and *reversurum*, the final future participle is chilling.

13–15 *ipse ... proiecit.* Striking though the figure is, especially her reappearance on the shore, the interest at the end of the story is the effect of the figure on Curtius Rufus' mind.

Lines 16–50

Pliny's second story is a conventional ghost story, featuring a haunted house, darkness, a sinister atmosphere and a classic ghost that all give the story-teller full rein.

17 *exponam ut accepi.* This may be true of the outline of the story, but the artistry with which the story is retold is Pliny's. A similar story is told by Lucian (*Philopseudes* 30-31) but he makes it sound less plausible by exaggerating and by adding lurid details.

17 *erat Athenis. erat* placed at the beginning and the scene set in a faraway place suggest that what follows is a fable. Cf. the opening of the story of Cupid and Psyche: '*erat in quadam civitate rex et regina*' (Apuleius *Metamorphoses* 4.28.1).

18–26 *per silentium ... timor erat.* This passage conveys the nature of the haunting in a series of lengthening descriptions, Pliny observing the psychological effects of the ghost on those who see it. The **sound** of the ghost's chains breaks the silence and gets closer (emphasised by the chiastic *longius primo/deinde proximo*); the ghost **appears** and is described; the **effects of his appearance** on the inhabitants, both immediate and lasting, are detailed.

21 *promissa ... capillo.* Ablatives of description without a conjunction (asyndeton).

21–22 *compedes ... catenas.* Ghosts in all ages traditionally wear chains, right up to Harry Potter, where among the gathering of ghosts in J. K. Rowling's *Harry Potter and the Chamber of Secrets* (London: Bloomsbury, 1998), there is 'a ragged man wearing chains' (chapter 8). Chains could be a sign that the man had been a prisoner or that he is weighed down by the deeds or events of life instead of being freed from them by death. This latter is spelt out by Marley's ghost in *A Christmas Carol* by Charles Dickens: the ghost's chains reflect his obsession with money, consisting of cash-boxes, keys, ledgers etc., and were, he says, forged by himself in his life through his failure to go about doing good to his fellow human beings. In Pliny's story, the chains appear to be real (see lines 44 and 47 ff. and notes), for whatever reason.

23 *inhabitantibus.* Dative of the person interested with *vigilabantur.*

27 *illi monstro.* The word can refer simply to a prodigy or manifestation, but here it clearly means a terrifying one. The description turns out to be ironic in the dénouement.

29 *Athenodorus.* Could be the historical Athenodorus of Tarsus, a teacher in the late Republic and friend of the emperor Augustus, or an unkown person of that name with connections with Athens. That he was a philopher explains his interest in the house, and perhaps his ability to remain calm.

33–34 *pugillares ... lumen, animum ... , manum.* The asyndeton in these matching sets of words perhaps conveys the business-like way in which Athenodorus gives his orders and then applies himself to his writing to eliminate the workings of his imagination. We are not told about his slaves' state of mind, but they are a reminder that he was not completely alone in the house.

36–39 *dein concuti ... audiri.* Historic infinitives, suggesting the usual pattern of events. The approaching sound of the ghost with his chains is heightened by Pliny's phrases *iam ut in limine, iam ut intra limen audiri.*

39–44 *respicit ... sequitur.* The switch to finite verbs here introduces the change in the turn of events, as Athenodorus' lack of fear impinges on the story and governs its remainder. Athenodorus shows his composure by asking the ghost to wait, but also by taking the ghost seriously.

44 *ibat ... vinculis.* The apparently real weight of the chains anticipates the finding of actual chains in lines 47–48.

47 *magistratus.* Pliny's expertise in government and the law ensures Athenodorus acts in accordance with the laws governing the dead: it was the magistrates' responsibility to investigate burials of unknown people especially if they had been carried out improperly inside a city instead of outside. No other rite or exorcism is required beyond burial to lay the ghost to rest.

49 *exesa ... vinculis.* The finding not only of fetters but also evidence of their having eaten into the bone is a further sign that these chains are perceived as real rather than symbolic, hard though it is to imagine scientifically.

Lines 51–65

This is likely to be regarded as the least plausible story, but also interesting as it concerned Pliny himself. It is tempting to think that the hair-cutting was a practical joke, but Pliny's possibly complex reasons for including it should not be ignored.

51 *et haec ... possum.* An elegant opening to the final story: others have persuaded Pliny, now he can persuade them.

52–53 *libertus ... quiescebat.* Pliny is anxious to represent his servant, a freedman, as a credible witness (*non inlitteratus*), as well as making clear that he was not alone, as in lines 58–59.

53–56 *is visus ... reperiuntur.* A supernatural mixture of dream and concrete evidence.

58 *(ita narrat).* On this second occasion, Pliny qualifies his belief: the evidence of slaves was not admissible in court unless they were tortured, and Pliny wants to pre-empt any accusation of gullibility. These dreams could apply to Pliny himself as the freedman and the slave were his (*meorum* line 65, 'my men' or 'my servants').

61 *non fui reus.* Anyone involved in opposing the emperor Domitian or any of those in favour with the emperor risked being accused, but while it is true that Pliny opposed Baebius Massa (7.33.7–9) and befriended Artemidorus (3.11.2–3), one of the philosophers exiled by Domitian in AD 93, he does not appear to have been seriously in danger of being a martyr of Domitian's rule. Sherwin-White (on 7.19.10) suggests that perhaps Pliny felt he should have been more courageous in defending those who had helped him to advance and who did fall foul of Domitian, and was tempted to magnify the danger he was in.

63 *Caro.* Mettius Carus, an informer under Domitian referred to in Pliny *Letters* 1.5.3 and 7.19.3.

65 *depulsi ... periculi.* The enclosing of the phrase *quod imminebat* indicates what it applies to.

Lines 66–71

A return to the tone of scientific enquiry, despite Pliny's artistry in telling the stories.

66–69 *eruditionem ... disputes.* Terms reflecting Sura's expertise, enquiring mind and weighing up of the evidence multiply.

- What part do the attitudes and expectations of the people who see the apparitions/dreams play in the stories?
- Compare the first story about Curtius Rufus with Tacitus' account in *Annals* 11.21.
- In commenting on the story of the haunted house, Sherwin-White, *The Letters of Pliny* (p. 437), says that Pliny's version 'would not disgrace the annals of a psychic research bureau'. Pick out parts of the narrative where Pliny gives an objective account.
- Read Lucian's version of the second story in translation (*Lover of Lies or the Sceptic*, e.g. translation by C. D. N. Costa in the Oxford World's Classics series, Oxford University Press 2005, pp. 175 f.) and compare it with Pliny's version.
- Do you think that Pliny particularly wants any of these stories to be true, and if so why?

Style

- Read aloud lines 9–11 (*perterrito ... moriturum*) to bring out the impact of the prophecy.
- Does Pliny's telling of the second story make the harmlessness of the ghost a surprise or a disappointment?

Further reading

- Sherwin-White, A. N. (ed.), *The Letters of Pliny: A Social and Historical Commentary* (Oxford: Oxford University Press, 1966). A large and thorough work, with articles on key aspects of Pliny's letters, which has informed subsequent studies but is useful to consult on points of detail.
- Sherwin-White, A. N. (ed.), *Fifty Letters of Pliny* (Oxford: Oxford University Press, 1969).
- Radice, B. (trans.), *The Letters of the Younger Pliny*, Penguin Classics, rev. repr. (Harmondsworth: Penguin, 1969).
- Walsh, P. G. (trans.), *Pliny the Younger: Complete Letters*, Oxford World's Classics (Oxford: Oxford University Press, 2006).

2. The mysterious death of Romulus—Livy *A History of Rome* 1.16

Rome was founded by Romulus, from whom it got its name. Together with his brother Remus, he was regarded as the son of Mars. The 'immortal works' mentioned in line 1 are summarised by Livy in the preceding chapter: using the arts of war and peace he established the city and secured its supremacy over neighbouring tribes. At the time of his death he was popular with the people and the army, but less so with the Senate .

Themes for exploration

- Deification and disappearing into heaven
- Political tensions
- Destiny of Rome

People and places

Romulus—mythical founder of Rome

Proculus—an otherwise unknown Roman senator

Notes on text

This episode is framed by Romulus' mysterious disappearance and his equally mysterious reappearance later to Proculus. Explanations for his disappearance play an important part in the story, one of which finally satisfies the people. Although not a long passage, it is quite dense with long sentences, and can usefully be divided into small sections.

Lines 1–4

Romulus' disappearance

1 *his ... operibus.* The first of a number of ablative absolutes which will need to be expanded in translation: 'when he had brought about these immortal achievements', referring to the summary of Romulus' works at the end of the previous chapter: securing the city by defeating her enemies and bringing about a peace which lasted for forty years. 'Immortal' because he was believed to be descended from Mars, but also looking forward to his divinity after death.

ad exercitum recensendum. Gerundive expressing purpose instead of *ut* + subjunctive.

2 *campo.* The Campus Martius, an open space near the Tiber to the north-west of the city, used for assemblies and military reviews as here.

3 *fragore tonitribusque.* To be taken together (hendiadys): 'the crashing of thunder'.

4 *contioni.* Dative of disadvantage following *abstulerit.*

Lines 5–9

Reactions to Romulus' disappearance

5–9 *Romana pubes ... obtinuit.* A long sentence beginning with the subject and ending with the main verb, with subordinate clauses and various phrases in between. One way of breaking this up is to translate the ablative absolute *sedato tandem pavore* as a main clause ('at length felt afraid no longer'). A new sentence could be begun at *ubi* (line 6), with the clauses beginning *etsi* and *tamen* dependent on *vidit.* The singular verbs and the feminine participle *icta* are accounted for by

Romana pubes remaining the subject throughout (the 'Roman youth' being the young soldiers who made up the army (*exercitus*) that Romulus was reviewing in line 1). See also versions of this sentence in the translations. However the sentence is broken up, students can be encouraged to see that the impact of this complex sentence is to roll into one the shifting and conflicting thoughts of the Roman youth.

8 *raptum.* Supply *esse.* *orbitatis.* A natural reaction to the loss of a 'father figure'. In the New Testament, Jesus Christ, anticipating his death and promising his coming again, says to his disciples, 'I will not leave you orphaned' (John 14.18, literally translated from the Greek in the New Revised Standard Version). In the Old Testament (Hebrew Scriptures), as Elijah ascends into heaven in a whirlwind, Elisha cries out 'Father, father!' (2 Kings 2.12).

Lines 9–15

Reasons for Romulus' disappearance

9–12 *deinde ... progeniem.* To recognise Romulus as a god and to worship him as king and father of Rome was to assume that the reason for his disappearance was his deification, a natural assumption given his divine parentage.

11 *pacem.* The divine favour that preserves the peace of his people.

12–15 *fuisse ... nobilitavit.* The other possible explanation for Romulus' disappearance. Livy has already said (chapter 15) that he was more popular with the people than with the senators. However, the degree of popular belief in Romulus' deification meant that the rumour of his assassination seeped out and was spread furtively, but overtly enough to cause hostility to the senators (line 17). Livy attributes the prevalence of the deification rumour to fear as well as admiration for Romulus.

14 *arguerent.* Subjunctive because the subject is indefinite.

Lines 15–25

Proculus' action and meeting with Romulus. The interest of this episode lies in the clues Livy gives to suggest that the meeting with Romulus was a skilful and strategic invention.

15–16 *consilio ... fides.* At the outset, Romulus' appearance, which added credibility to his deification, is presented as a plan or strategy on Proculus' part.

17–18 *gravis ... auctor.* Proculus' reputation is stressed but is it a reputation for diplomacy or for truth?

19 *parens.* The term would appeal particularly to those who felt 'orphaned'.

21 *horrore.* The usual response to an encounter with a god or any supernatural manifestation. Cf. 4.10 in this section, and Virgil, e.g. *Aeneid* 4.280. Here it makes Proculus' experience convincing.

22–25 *caelestes ... posse.* The psychology of Romulus' message, delivered in the jussive subjunctives *colant, sciant* and *tradant*, is shrewd in uniting the Romans not only in their belief in him as a god but also in a god-given destiny requiring them to build on his foundation and look confidently to the future.

25 *haec ... abiit.* Proculus makes sure that Romulus' convincing return to heaven is recorded.

Lines 26–28

Result of Proculus' action

26 *mirum ... fuerit. fidei* is a partitive genitive with *quantum, haec* is the object of (*illi viro*) *nuntianti.*

27 *apud plebem exercitumque.* Livy makes clear that it was the most volatile sections of the city who were consoled and satisfied with Proculus' story.

Further teaching suggestions

Content

- Imagine you are investigating the disappearance of Romulus. What could you put in the following table about suspects?

Suspect	Motive	Opportunity
The senators		
The army		
Romulus himself		

- Compare other 'ascensions', to see what is similar to Romulus' disappearance and what is different. See 2 Kings 2.2.1–18 (Elijah); Acts of the Apostles 1.6–11 (Jesus Christ). Mohammed also made a mysterious journey to heaven though not at his death.

- Write in English the prayer to Romulus suggested by the ideas and phrases in lines 10–12 (*deum ... progeniem*).

Style

- Read aloud lines 5–9 (*Romana pubes ... obtinuit*), and see how you can bring out the way Livy indicates the different moods of the Roman youth.

Further reading

- Gould, H. E. and Whiteley, J. E. (eds.), *Livy: Book 1*, Latin Texts (London: Methuen, 1951; London: Bristol Classical Press/Duckworth, 2004).

- de Sélincourt, A. (trans.), preface by Oakley, S. *Livy: The Early History of Rome*, Penguin Classics (Harmondsworth: Penguin, 2002).

- Luce, T. J. (trans.), *Livy: The Rise of Rome Books 1–5*, Oxford World's Classics (Oxford: Oxford University Press, 1998).

3. Omens, portents and the murder of Julius Caesar— Suetonius *Divine Julius* 81, 88

In the early history of Rome, the last king became cruel and tyrannical, and was assassinated, leaving the Romans with a fear of absolute rule. Centuries later, the military and political strength of Julius Caesar convinced a group of senators that too much power was concentrated in the hands of one man. His conquests, the lavish entertainments he had put on to celebrate his triumphs and his many projects in Rome made him popular with the army and people, hut he was now permanent consul and dictator, and there was a rumour that he was to be made king at the meeting of the Senate on the Ides of March in 44 BC. This spurred on the conspirators, who decided that he had to be assassinated for the sake of the Republic. Among them was a friend of Caesar, Marcus Junius Brutus*, who was the descendant of one of the men who had killed the last king and was persuaded that he should follow his ancestor in restoring liberty to the Roman people by leading the conspiracy with Cassius. Another Brutus, Decimus Brutus, was also among the conspirators and persuaded Caesar to go to the Senate.

Themes for exploration
- Portents as warnings
- Deification
- Appearance of heavenly signs

People and places

Julius Caesar—outstanding statesman and general of the late Roman Republic, assassinated by senators because of suspcions that he was aiming for absolute rule

River Rubicon—river forming the boundary between Gaul and Italy. In crossing it in 49 BC with his army Caesar precipitated the Civil War between himself and Pompey the Great. See section 6.4.

Spurinna—a haruspex or soothsayer

Calpurnia—wife of Julius Caesar

Decimus Brutus—a conspirator. See footnote on the Brutus family.

Augustus—Octavian, great-nephew and heir of Julius Caesar. He took the name Augustus when he became the first Roman emperor.

Notes on text

Lines 1–12

One portent would have been ominous, but the number of portents seems to be in proportion to Caesar's fame and the violence of his death.

1–2 *equorum greges ... consecrarat*. This is not recorded by Suetonius in his account of the crossing of the Rubicon.

4 *Spurinna*. A key figure, also highlighted by Shakespeare in *Julius Caesar*. As a haruspex he may have delivered this warning when he had inspected the entrails of the animal sacrificed by Caesar.

6 *cum laureo ramulo*. Denoting victory, appropriate to Caesar. *Pompeianae curiae*. Ironically, the Senate was to meet on the Campus Martius (see 6.2) in the theatre built by Pompey, whom Caesar had defeated in the Civil War.

8 *discerpserunt*. For the violence of the image cf. section 6.2, where the same word is used of the rumours of the true cause of Romulus' disappearance (line 13). This may prompt discussion about similarities between Caesar and Romulus.

---

* The Brutus family was ancient and there are a number of people called Brutus in Roman history. The picture in the Students' Book does not show the Decimus Brutus mentioned by Suetonius, but might be an imaginative portrait of the Brutus who ended the monarchy and was the first consul: the bronze bust conveys the stern, upright realism associated with the heroes of the Roman Republic that Caesar's assassins claimed to be restoring.

8–10 *ipse … iungere*. Compared with the portents described above and his wife's dream, the peaceful quality of Caesar's dreams (tinged with delusions of grandeur) can perhaps be related to chapter 87 (not included in the *Anthology* passage), where Suetonius reports theories that Caesar did not want to live longer, with failing health and the constant threat of attack, and that the assassination was the kind of quick, sudden end that he wished for.

10–12 *Calpurnia … patuerunt*. Plutarch in his account (63–64) makes more of these portents, especially Calpurnia's dream of the murdered Caesar in her arms. Here Suetonius adds the detail about the pediment. These were normally restricted to temples, but the right to have one in his house was one of the privileges granted to Caesar. A coin commemorating Caesar's deification shows a comet on a pediment, which refers to the temple dedicated to him but might also recall the grant of a pediment. For another troubled Roman wife see the gospel according to Saint Matthew chapter 27 verse 19 (the wife of Pilate warning him about Christ as a result of a dream). The spontaneous opening of the doors has no obvious interpretation but increases the sense of eeriness and insecurity.

Lines 12–21

Caesar eventually decides to go. The picture at the front of this section in the Students' Book (p. 125) illustrates his progress to the Senate, and students can identify the various characters.

12–13 *ob infirmam valetudinem*. In chapter 45 Suetonius states that Caesar enjoyed good health but became prone to fainting fits, nightmares and epilepsy. See above on lines 8–10.

14 *Decimo Bruto adhortante*. Here Decimus Brutus concentrates on the expectations of the Senate. In Plutarch's version (64) he also makes light of the omens and particularly Calpurnia's dreams, but ingeniously suggests that if the day is in fact inauspicious, Caesar should go and tell the senators himself.

15 *quinta … hora*. This was about 11 o'clock, late in the day for the Senate to meet.

16–18 *progressus … tenebat*. The almost parenthetical way in which the document detailing the conspiracy is handed over compounds Caesar's own unwitting disregard for it.

19–21 *spreta religione … praeterisse*. Caesar's bravado gets the better of his doubts about the omens, but he speaks too soon, in the famous exchange with Spurinna.

Lines 22–25

A comet appears to be a sign of Caesar's deification.

22–23 *stella crinita*. The names of the constellations are witness to ancient stories about people turning into stars. For another reference to the comet see section 6.7 line 33.

> *Further teaching suggestions*
>
> **Content**
>
> - Different groups of students could read chapters 63 and 64 of Plutarch's *Life of Julius Caesar*, and Shakespeare *Julius Caesar* Act 3 scene 1 and compare them with Suetonius.
>
> - How might the story have been given interest and suspense if the portents of Caesar's death had not been included?
>
> **Style**
>
> - Read chapter 65 of Plutarch's *Life of Julius Caesar* (about the attempt to inform him of the conspiracy) and compare Suetonius' version. How does each one convey the suspense?

Further reading

- Edwards, C. (trans.), *Suetonius: Lives of the Caesars*, Oxford World's Classics (Oxford:Oxford University Press, 2000). Includes a section in the Introduction on omens and portents (pp. xviii f.).

- Graves, R. (trans.) and Rives, J., *Suetonius: The Twelve Caesars*, Penguin Classics (Harmondsworth: Penguin 2007).

- Warner, R. (trans.) and Seager, R. (ed.), *Plutarch: Fall of the Roman Republic*, Penguin Classics (Harmondsworth: Penguin, 2006).

- Bradley, P. *Ancient Rome: Using Evidence* (Edward Arnold (Australia) PTY Ltd 1990. Repr. Cambridge: Cambridge University Press, 2000). Detailed knowledge of the historical background is *not* required for the OCR GCSE in Latin, but this book is useful for reference or for students who wish to pursue questions about Caesar.

4. Caesar crosses the Rubicon—Lucan *Civil War* 1.183–227 (abridged)

As proconsul of Gaul, Caesar won many battles on behalf of Rome. His supporters wanted him either to be allowed to stand for election as consul or to retain command of his armies. With relations between him and Pompey worsening, he declined to give up his command and lay down his arms unless Pompey did the same. When his demand was refused by the Senate, in 49 BC he crossed the River Rubicon from Gaul into Italy with his army. Because it was illegal for a Roman general to enter Italy from his province at the head of an army, Caesar declared war on the Senate by this action and started the Civil War between himself and Pompey. Lucan's poem about the Civil War is written from an anti-Caesar standpoint, perhaps influenced by the example of the emperor Nero as a bad absolute ruler.

Themes for exploration
- Personification
- Ambition and destiny
- Conquest and images of conquest

Metre—Hexameters

People and places

Julius Caesar—outstanding statesman and general of the late Roman Republic, eventually assassinated in 44 BC by senators because of suspcions that he was aiming for absolute rule. One of his greatest achievements was his conquest of the province of Gaul, from which he is returning in this passage.

Alps—mountain range separating Gaul from Italy

River Rubicon—river forming the boundary between Gaul and Italy. By crossing it in 49 BC with his army Caesar precipitated the Civil War between himself and Pompey the Great.

Tarpeian Rock—the rock on the SW corner of the Capitoline Hill from which traitors were thrown

The Thunderer=Jupiter

Phrygian household gods—brought form Troy (in Phrygia) by Aeneas: Caesar claimed descent from Iulus ('*gentis Iuleae*'), Aeneas' son.

Quirinus=Romulus—mythical founder of Rome. For his disappearance see section 6.2

Alba (Longa)—the mother city of Rome in Latium (*Latiaris* in the text)

Vestal—the title given to the virgin priestresses who tended the fire sacred to Vesta, goddess of the hearth

Hesperia—the 'western land', i.e. Italy

Fortuna—Fortune, personified as a goddess. Cf section 6.6

Notes on text

Lines 1–23

The appearance of the image of Rome at the Rubicon indicates that for Lucan civil war was already Caesar's intention.

1 *gelidas ... Alpes*. Like Hannibal (section 4.3), an enemy of Rome, Caesar has 'conquered' the icy Alps in his journey back from Gaul, and is now about to 'conquer' Italy.

4–8 *ingens ... loqui*. The Students' Book offers guidance with the convoluted phrases of this long sentence, which needs to be broken at *crines*, and the following infinitives *adstare* and *loqui* taken as finite verbs. For the larger-than-life female apparition representing a nation cf. 6.1 line 8. Here the figure is shown prophetically in mourning with a sad expression and torn hair, as if Caesar's violation of the law had already taken place. She addresses the whole army, not only Caesar, because Lucan has portrayed Caesar's army as being strongly in favour of his marching on Italy in the previous lines. *turrigero ... vertice*. Because she represented a city. *clara per obscuram ... noctem*. Lucan puts the contrasting *clara* and *obscuram* together, creating a striking, potentially cinematic image.

10–12 *tum ... ripa*. The characteristic shock and dread at seeing a divine apparition, often involving *horror*. Cf. 6.2 line 21.

12 *in extrema ... ripa*. The figure of Rome appears to make a last-minute plea.

14 *Tarpeia de rupe*. Associated with the mythical Tarpeia who betrayed Rome to the Gauls. In view of Lucan's perspective, the reference is ironic as Caesar was about to commit treason by marching on his own country. Jupiter the Thunderer (Tonans) looks out from the rock as it was on the SW corner of the Capitoline Hill where the Temple of Jupiter was.

14 *Tonans ... Roma*. Caesar mentions all the key deities associated with Rome, going back to the household gods brought from Troy, and including the spirit of Rome, in an all-embracing prayer. In this way he presents himself as a citizen in defiance of Rome's gibe in line 10 (*si cives*). *rapti ... Quirini*. As described in 6.2. The *Vestales ... foci* (poetic plural) were guarded by the Vestal Virgins.

20 *tuus*. Caesar presents himself as the warrior and servant of Rome.

21 *ille*. A general statement or more likely, in view of the emphatic repetition, referring to the Senate and the consuls.

22 *tumidum*. The small river was in flood because of the winter rains and melting snow, as Lucan explains in the following lines (omitted), but there may also be a hint that even the river was trying to resist Caesar's illegal passage.

22–23 *inde ... propere*. In Suetonius' account (*Caesar* 32), this is the point at which a divine figure appears, this time leading him on.

24 *superato*. The river is 'defeated' as were the Alps (line 1).

25 *vetitis ... arvis*. 'Forbidden' only because he has crossed into them with his army.

26 *temerata ... iura*. Further irony, as Lucan sees Caesar seeking redress for the 'violated laws' by breaking the law himself. In his own account (*Civil War* 1.5–8), Caesar claimed to be seeking peace, and portrays the Senate as raising troops for Pompey. The 'laws' mentioned may be a reference to the apparent snub to the tribunes who were resisted in their attempts to read out Caesar's messages and were evicted from the Senate in defiance of their rights and authority. They reported this to Caesar, giving him his pretext for action.

27 *procul ... sunto*. The 'treaties' referred to are probably the alliance between Caesar, Pompey and Crassus (the First Triumvirate which ended with Crassus' death in 53 BC) and the marriage of Caesar's daughter Julia to Pompey. She died in 54 BC. The phrase *procul ... sunto* has an archaic, quasi-religious tone that Lucan may have intended to sound blasphemous in connection with breaking treaties.

Further teaching suggestions

Content

- How effective is the figure of Rome in representing resistance to Caesar?

- 🔊 Listen to the passage on the audio CD (track 42). Do you think the reader implies that Caesar's dread was genuine or long-lasting (lines 10–12)?

- How convincing is Caesar's justification of his action?

- Compare Caesar's own account of crossing the Rubicon (Caesar *Civil War* 1.5–8) and Suetonius' account (*Caesar* 31–32).

Style

- How does irony contribute to a negative view of Caesar in the passage?

Further reading

- Braund, S.H. (trans.), *Lucan: Civil War*, Oxford World's Classics (Oxford: Oxford University Press, 2000). Includes a section in the Introduction on the supernatural in Lucan, with a useful summary of this passage (p. xxv).

- Bradley, P. *Ancient Rome: Using Evidence* (Edward Arnold (Australia) PTY Ltd 1990. Repr. Cambridge: Cambridge University Press, 2000). Detailed knowledge of the historical background is *not* required for the OCR GCSE in Latin, but this book is useful for reference or for students who wish to pursue questions about Caesar.

- Forrest, M., Heatley, E., Hughes, M. and Widdess M., *Pompey and Caesar*, compiled from Plutarch, Suetonius and other ancient sources, Cambridge School Classics Project *Classical Studies 13–16* Book III and *Teacher's Handbook* (Cambridge: Cambridge University Press, 1986 OP.) Translated source material including passages referred to above for comparison with Lucan.

🔊 5. Praying for profit—Persius *Satires* 2.44–52

It could be said that 'the Romans' practised many strange religious rituals. This short passage shows that as in any society there were differing views, or that at the very least there was scepticism about excessive or superstitious use of sacrifice and haruspicy. It takes the common satirical form of the poet interrogating a person who is presented as acting absurdly. The *Satire* from which this extract is taken has a strongly moralising tone, ridiculing superstition and, at the end, urging that a righteous heart, a` pure mind and a noble soul are the best offerings.

Themes for exploration

- Divination as superstition
- Irony of spending money looking for wealth

Metre—Hexameters

People and places

Mercury—god of profit and business

Penates—household gods

Notes on text

Lines 1–8

1 *rem ... bove*. The theme is the paradox of trying to accumulate wealth by sacrificing it.

2 *arcessis fibra*. The bathos of grandly summoning the god with a single liver, i.e. by sacrificing and employing the haruspex.

2–3 *da ... da*. The urgent repeated petition of prayer.

3–4 *quo ... liquescant*. The implication is that as fast as the gods grant him increase, his flocks and herds are sacrificed. *tibi*. Dative of the person interested, expressing possession.

5 *vincere*. A strong word, suggesting the man's determination to win over the god by whatever means.

6–7 *iam ... iam*. As his wealth disappears the deluded man sees it increase.

7–8 *donec ... imo*. The man's last coin, personified, recognises the absurdity of the situation although it escapes the man himself.

Further teaching suggestions

Content

- Do you think the poet is satirising the man for being superstitious, over-zealous, or for worshipping the gods at all?

Style

- 🔊 How does the poet's use of repetition add to the effect? (Listening to the audio CD (track 43) is a way of alerting students to the repetition.)

Further reading

- Ramsay, G. G. (trans.), *Juvenal and Persius*, Loeb Classical Library (Cambridge, Mass., Harvard University Press and London: William Heinemann Ltd, 1918; rev. repr. 1969).

- Rudd, N. (trans.), *The Satires of Horace and Persius*, Penguin Classics (Harmondsworth: Penguin, 2005).

- Conington, J. (trans. and ed.), *Persius: Satires*, Classic Commentaries (Bristol: Bristol Classical Press, 1998).

◉ 6. A sign from heaven—Horace *Odes* 1.34

Because Horace often writes in the first person, there are differing views about the extent to which we can find actual autobiographical information in his poetry. He certainly uses scenes from life though not necessarily his own. But being a Roman poet writing with a strong sense of genre and detailed knowledge of those who wrote before him in the same genre, he also draws on the themes of the Greek lyric poets in his *Odes*, or Lucilius in his *Satires*.

However, while remaining cautious about whether he is describing an actual incident here, we can be confident this poem does reflect the consistent strand of Epicureanism in Horace's poetry, expressed as doubt that immortality offers any permanent benefits as compared with the present life and, of relevance here, disbelief in the omnipotence of the gods and their concern with human life. This disbelief is challenged by the awe-inspiring glimpse of Jupiter described. But if the poet now sees the god and Fortune in control after all, he reflects that human hopes are still precarious when individuals can be either exalted or cast down. There the poem ends, with no hint of a 'conversion', and Epicurean ideas continue to make an appearance in Horace's works.

Themes for exploration
- Religious belief and the numinous
- Divine dispensation

Metre—Alcaics

People and places

Diespiter = Jupiter

River Styx—one of the rivers of the Underworld

Taenarum—a place in the south of the Peloponnese in Greece where a cave was believed to be the entrance to the Underworld

the boundary marked by Atlas—i.e. the limit of the known world

Fortuna—Fortune personified as a goddess. Cf. section 6.4.

Notes on text

1 *parcus … infrequens.* Thrifty (*parcus*) in the amount of worship he offered, perhaps literally thrifty as sacrifices were expensive, but the word also conveys a grudging attitude to religious practice. Reinforced by *infrequens*.

2–3 *insanientis … erro.* The word-order stresses the paradox of a 'wisdom' that is 'mad' and an 'expert' who 'wanders'. *sapientiae.* The word used by Epicureans of their philosophy.

3–5 *nunc … relictos.* The poet's laxness in religion is presented as a lapse from an earlier attitude of greater devotion to which he must now make the return journey. The idea is carried over into the next verse, so that the appearance of Diespiter is all the more abrupt.

5 *namque.* A word that occurs more commonly in prose to introduce a reason or explanation. *Diespiter.* An archaic form of the name Jupiter, in keeping with the supposed return to traditional religion..

6–8 *igni corusco … tonantes … equos.* Horace uses indirect expressions (periphrasis) to refer to the lightning and thunder.

7 *plerumque.* Another prosaic word after the poetic line 2, which introduces a scientific tone: observation suggests that *as a general rule* lightning and thunder occur in conjunction with clouds. This is appropriate to an Epicurean who would look for physical rather than divine causes for natural phenomena (e.g. Lucretius 6.160–218 on thunder, and 379–422 where divine causes are ridiculed).

9 *quo.* Grammatically the antecedent is *currus*, standing for the whole impact caused by Jupiter's passing through the clear sky with its attendant lightning and crack of thunder.

9–12 *bruta … concutitur.* Horace selects physical features of the earth (*tellus, flumina*), and names that evoke its depths in the Underworld (*Styx, sedes Taenari*) and distant regions (*Atlanteus finis*). Together these indicate how the force of the lightning and thunder seems to affect the whole earth physically (*concutitur*), and has a humbling effect on those who witness it. The passage moves the poem abruptly from the self-deprecatory tone of the opening and paves the way for the next transition to the general thought inspired by the particular incident.

12–17 *valet … gaudet*. Sudden change of fortune, often with a moral theme, is a common theme in religion, as well as in classical literature (especially common in Greek tragedy, e.g. Oedipus, Agamemnon). In keeping with the more general observation, *deus* replaces *Diespiter*, and in turn *deus* gives way to *Fortuna* or Fate. The progression broadens the canvas of the poem, but 'the god' and Fortuna are close. There is perhaps a suggestion that the god deliberately reverses people's situations, while Fortune merely changes them randomly, for her own gratification.

Further reading

- Quinn. K., *Horace: Odes* (London: Macmillan Educational 1980; London: Bristol Classical Press/Duckworth, 1996).

- Michie, J. (trans.), *The Odes of Horace* (Harmondsworth: Penguin Classics,1964). Fairly free translation into verse, preserving some of the original metres, and notes. Out of print.

- West, D. (trans.), *Horace: The Complete Odes and Epodes*. Oxford World's Classics, (Oxford: Oxford University Press, 1997). A more literal translation than Michie's, with notes and biographical information.

- Fraenkel, E., *Horace* (Oxford: Oxford University Press, 1957). Still a standard work.

Further teaching suggestions

Content

- Horace squeezes a lot of content into 16 lines. What do you think is the main theme and how do the others contribute to it?

- 🔊 Listen to the audio CD (track 44). How does the reading bring out the changes of mood in the poem?

- How does Horace use images to convey his meaning? (See lines 3–5, 7–8 and 14–16.)

Style

- Look at the Latin and compare the following translations of the phrase *insanientis dum sapientiae consultus erro* (lines 2–3):

  (a) I …
      … must now confess
      Myself professor in pure foolishness
      (Michie)

  (b) a wanderer expert
      in a crazy wisdom (West)

⏺ 7. The shield of Aeneas—Virgil *Aeneid* 8.608–731 (abridged)

With Aeneas in Italy, where Rome will eventually be founded, his mother persuades her husband Vulcan to forge new armour to help Aeneas in his wars with the local Latin tribes (Vulcan is described in 8.407–415; see section 1.3). The episode is derived from the armour Hephaestus makes for Achilles in Homer *Iliad* 18. There the scenes on the shield depict Greek life, but Virgil uses the shield in his patriotic epic to reveal the history of the future Rome. This extract is about the most recent historical events on the shield: the battle of Actium in which Octavian (who became the emperor Augustus) defeated Antony and Cleopatra and gained control of the eastern empire. What is presented to Aeneas as prophecy that he cannot fully understand (*rerum ... ignarus* line 82) is a glorification of Rome's recent past and Augustus' role in it. It confirms to Aeneas the destiny of the city he is to found which he was shown first by his father Anchises on a visit to the Underworld (*Aeneid* 6), another example of prophecy taking the form of a vivid narrative of what for the reader are past events. In addition to the narrative itself, a number of phrases link Aeneas to later history. These are in ***bold italic*** in the following notes to facilitate their collection.

Themes for exploration

- Divine favour
- Miraculous gifts
- History as the future
- Propaganda
- Winners and losers
- Colour and movement

Metre—Hexameters

People and places

Aeneas—Trojan prince, destined by the gods to sail for Italy and found a settlement there, leading eventually to the founding of Rome by his descendants

Venus (also Cytherea)—daughter of Jupiter, goddess of love and beauty and mother of Aeneas

Laurentines (a tribe of Latium); Turnus (prince of the Rutulians)—enemies Aeneas will meet when he lands in Italy

Ascanius (also Iulus)—son of Aeneas

Actium—on the west coast of Greece, the site of the sea-battle in which Octavian defeated Antony and Cleopatra

Leucate—a promontory near Actium

Augustus Caesar—Octavian, great-nephew and heir of Julius Caesar. He took the name Augustus later when he became the first Roman emperor

Marcus Vipsanius Agrippa—Octavian's general

Antony—Mark Antony, former ally of Caesar and then of Octavian who became estranged from him because of his relationship with Cleopatra and his support for her and her territorial interests

Egypt—ruled by Cleopatra (*Aegyptia coniunx*)

Bactra—in central Asia

Anubis—Egyptian god with the head of a jackal

Neptune—god of the sea

Minerva—goddess of wisdom and warfare

Mars (Mavors)—god of war

Furies, Discord—personifications of agents of warfare

Bellona—goddess of war (sister of Mars)

Apollo (Phoebus)—god of music and archery, who was on the side of the Trojans

Sabaeans—a tribe of Arabia

Nile—river of Egypt

Numidians—nomadic tribes of Africa

Mulciber = Vulcan—blacksmith god

Lelages and Carians—tribes of Asia Minor

Gelonians and Dahae—tribes of Scythia

Morini—tribe of northern Gaul

Euphrates (Mesopotamia), Rhine (modern Germany), Araxes (Armenia)—rivers

Notes on text

Lines 1–22

The armour is given to Aeneas by his mother and is described. Aeneas' wonder and admiration.

1–2 *at Venus ... aderat*. The clouds (*aetherios ... nimbos*) contrast with the radiance of the goddess (*candida*), but also conceal her arrival: Aeneas only sees her when she is actually present (*aderat*). Cf. line 4 *ultro*, which implies a sudden or surprise event.

2 *in valle reducta*. A secluded place for this divine encounter, but also the setting for Aeneas' view on the shield of Rome's future. Similarly, the souls of the future great Romans wait in the Underworld in a *valle reducta* (*Aeneid* 6.703).

5–6 *perfecta ... munera. perfecta munera* go together (nominative) while *promissa arte* go together (ablative). The phrase is a useful demonstration of the use of quantities to determine case endings in poetry: the long and short endings can be heard on the audio CD. The literal 'promised skill of my husband' in the gloss could be improved with a phrase such as 'the skill my husband promised'. The point is that it was the *skill* that was promised, i.e. Vulcan promised to use his skill in making the armour.

6–7 *Laurentes ... Turnum*. The purpose of the arms is spelt out. The *Aeneid* ends with the death of Turnus at Aeneas' hand.

9 *adversa ... quercu*. Augustus had been given an oak wreath in 27 BC, an award given for saving the lives of fellow-citizens. The chiastic arrangement of *arma/radiantia* and *adversa/quercu* heightens the importance of both the arms and the oak.

10 *deae ... honore*. The paraphrase in the gloss suggests taking the phrase as a hendiadys. If they are translated separately as 'the gifts of the goddess/his divine mother and the great honour', the sense of honour is still closely related to the divine gifts.

13 *flammasque vomentem*. Connects Aeneas with Augustus; see 32–33.

14 *fatiferum ... ensem*. A grim prophecy of the slaughter that has to be accomplished by this sword to win the land in the battles that dominate the rest of the poem, culminating in the death of Turnus.

14–16 *loricam ... refulget*. The description of the piece of armour that enhances Aeneas' size and shape as he is viewed in the distance on the battle field. The breastplate is huge (*ingentem*) because Aeneas himself is, having heroic stature.

18 *clipei ... textum*. At the same time as the oak-leaf crown for saving citizens' lives (see on line 9), Augustus was also given a golden shield. This would probably have been in the minds of Virgil's contemporaries as much as the shield given to Achilles in *Iliad* 18. *textum* implies the craftsmanship and 'interweaving' of the stories. The shield is the last in the list of armour, because of its importance but also because the description of it can then follow straight on. Of the shield, Virgil says (ironically or modestly in the light of the following 100 lines devoted to the shield) that it 'cannot be described' (*enarrabile*).

19 *res ... triumphos*. Embraces the earliest history before Rome was built right through to Augustus' triumphs depicted in the centre of the shield.

20–21 *haud ... ignipotens*. Vulcan is compared comically in 8.407–415 to a housewife (see section 1.3), but here he is knowledgeable and prophetic. His knowledge (*haud ... ignarus*) contrasts with Aeneas' ignorance (*rerum ... ignarus*, line 82). See Gransden's note on the shield for the idea that Vulcan 'stands for the figure of the poet himself' (p. 162) in respect of both insight and craftsmanship.

22 *stirpis ab Ascanio*. According to one genealogy, Romulus was descended from Ascanius through his mother's line.

Lines 23–80

The centrepiece of the shield described

The battle of Actium was the outcome of worsening relations between Mark Antony and Octavian (the future emperor Augustus, and referred to by Virgil as Augustus in this passage and in these notes). Antony held power in the East, where he and Cleopatra of Egypt had formed an alliance, while Octavian was powerful in Rome and in the West. Despite a marriage alliance (Antony married Octavian's sister in 40 BC), the power-sharing broke down. The battle of Actium was fought in 31 BC, giving Octavian control of the East as well as the West and consolidating his position as the most powerful ruler in Rome. The battle was therefore an obvious centrepiece for the shield of Aeneas.

After a brief overview of the scene (lines 23–29), the description falls into sections, the episodes involving Antony and Cleopatra sandwiched between those involving Augustus, with the battle of fleets and the gods in the middle.

Augustus Caesar's fleet,
starting at *hinc* (line 30)

The **fleet of Antony and Cleopatra**,
starting with a corresponding *hinc* (line 37)

The **battle of the fleets**
is engaged (lines 41–49)

The **battle of the gods**,
and their **role in the battle** (lines 50–57)

The **flight of the eastern forces**,
and **retreat of Cleopatra** to the **Nile**
(lines 57–65)

Augustus' triumph at **Rome**:
sacrifices and **conquered peoples**
(lines 66–80)

Lines 23–29

23 *haec inter*. Referring to the 8 scenes of earlier Roman history depicted round the shield.

23–26 *haec ... secabant*. An outstanding example of how the scenes on the shield are both engraved in metal but also 'brought to life' as colourful moving images. Cf. *auro ... effulgere fluctus*, line 29 below

27 *classes aeratas*. Probably not the metal of the shield this time but the bronze on the ships, in particular the bronze 'beaks' with which they rammed enemy vessels. Cf. *rostrata corona* below (line 36). But the adjective also adds to the gleaming, metallic appearance of the shield.

Actia bella. Virgil makes Aeneas visit Actium himself to hold games there and dedicate a shield in the temple of Apollo (3.278–288).

29 *Leucaten*. Here equated by Virgil with Actium; in both places there were temples of Apollo, and there was a tradition that Aeneas had founded temples to Venus, making a link between Augustus at Actium and Aeneas.

Lines 30–36

31 *cum patribus populoque*. In one line Virgil makes clear the extent of Augustus' support: unlike Julius Caesar and Romulus before him, he was backed by the Senate as well as the people.

penatibus ... dis. In the same line Virgil succinctly indicates also Augustus' divine support: the Roman 'household gods' were brought from the defeated Troy, but now support Augustus on the winning side, while he is also championed by the 'great gods', the Graeco-Roman gods (see lines 51–52), or perhaps Castor and Pollux (known as 'great gods'), shown on Augustus' Ara Pacis with Aeneas sacrificing to them. The impact of the gods is heightened by the monosyllabic ending.

32 *geminas ... tempora*. Cf. line 13. Either Augustus was also wearing a helmet with fiery crests, or the flames in this case formed an aura of divine favour, in conjunction with the comet associated with Julius Caesar, Augustus' adoptive father (*patrium ... sidus*; see passage 3 in this section). Cf. the similar portents bestowed on Ascanius in *Aeneid* 2.682 ff., and the description of Romulus in *Aeneid* 6.779 f.

34 *ventis ... secundis*. Like Augustus, Agrippa is supported by the gods, but also by the winds as befits a naval commander.

35–36 *arduus ... corona*. Agrippa is described in three lines parallel to the description of Augustus.

36 *tempora ... corona*. The *corona navalis* or *rostrata* was a rare honour conferred on Agrippa for his defeat of Sextius Pompeius in 36 BC. Its decoration was derived from the rostra or beaks of ships. Here the epithet *rostrata* is transferred to *tempora*, and the phrase *belli insigne superbum* is explanatory, an accusative in apposition to the sentence: ' ... whose temples blaze with the beaks of the Naval Crown, the proud decoration of war'.

Lines 37–40

37–40 *hinc ... coniunx.* Four lines describing Antony and Cleopatra correspond to the description of Augustus, also beginning with *hinc.* *ope barbarica*, contrasting with *Italos* in line 30. *victor.* Antony had come from Parthia where he had been fighting a campaign. The exotic places and the plurals in these lines build up a picture of a motley and extravagantly equipped force compared with Augustus' solidly Italian one. The east is emphasised by the use of both *Aurorae* and *Orientis.*

40 (nefas) Aegyptia coniunx. Antony's dalliance with Cleopatra is likely to have been in the minds of Virgil's readers when they read *Aeneid* 4, where Aeneas himself is lured away from his duty by Dido, another African queen (manipulated by Juno however). Despite Antony's marriage to Octavia (he did not divorce her until 32 BC), he recognised the children he had by Cleopatra, and gave them and her parts of Roman territory in a bid to restore the Egyptian kingdom. The Augustan poets never refer to her by name, reflecting Roman suspicion and hatred, not without fascination.

Lines 41–49

41–49 *una ... angues.* The scene, technically engraved on metal, has now become cinematic.

41 *ruere ... spumare.* Historic infinitives.

45 *turritis puppibus.* Antony's ships were particularly massive owing to the towers built on to the decks. See Fordyce.

47 *arva ... rubescunt.* Another line where noticing the quantities ensures the right words are taken together. *nova ... caede.* 'New' or 'fresh' because it is just beginning, or because two Romans are fighting each other, recalling the Civil War (cf. *Discordia*, line 54).

48 *sistro.* Another gibe at the exotic forces of Antony and Cleopatra: Roman troops would have been marshalled by a trumpet (see picture on p. 148).

49 *geminos ... angues.* A sign of death (twin snakes were sent to kill Hercules), but the irony here is that the snake was a symbol of Egyptian royalty, and the story was that Cleopatra killed herself with an asp. On the shield the snakes are behind her, so her fate is unforeseen.

Lines 50–57

50–52 *omnigenumque ... tenent.* The animal-headed gods of the Egyptians (*monstra*) and the Roman gods do not only aid their respective sides but engage in battle themselves.

53 *caelatus ferro.* A reminder that it is a metal shield on which the scene is depicted.

53–54 *Dirae ... Discordia.* The Furies and Discord appear on the threshold of the Underworld (*Aeneid* 6.280). Discord's cloak is symbolically torn.

56–57 *Actius ... Apollo desuper. Actius* because he had a temple at Actium, and to emphasise the battle of Actium (cf. *Actia bella*, line 27). The climax of the battle for gods and men: Apollo, guardian of both the Trojans and Augustus, bends his bow dramatically from above with a strong break in the sense and the rhythm.

Lines 57–65

57–58 *omnis ... omnis ... omnes ... Sabaei.* The completeness of the rout of the eastern forces is conveyed in a threefold sentence with each phrase beginning with forms of the same word (tricolon with anaphora). The different nationalities also convey the extent of the defeat.

59–60 *ipsa ... funes.* The alliteration of *v*, in these lines, carrying on from *vertebant* in line 58, heightens the dramatic effect, while the repetition in *iam iamque* increases the sense of urgency. Cf. passage 5 in this section.

60–65 *vela dare ... victos.* The flight of Cleopatra, and the pathos of her retreat into the bosom of the Nile.

60 *vela ... funes*. Logically she could set sail only after she had let out the sheets, but the two actions are dependent on each other and seen as one action.

61–65 *illam ... victos*. The phrases *illam pallentem morte futuram, maerentem ... Nilum* and *vocantem ... victos* arouse sympathy for the defeated queen and her people, all the more striking for the disdain of lines 37, 40 and 48. In this Cleopatra joins other enemies in the *Aeneid* who unexpectedly attract sympathy, especially Dido in Book 4 and Turnus in the closing lines of Book 12. Dido is also described as *pallida morte futura* (*Aen.* 4.644).

Lines 66–80

66 *at Caesar*. *at* marks a decisive change of person and scene, from the defeated Cleopatra finding solace in Egypt to the victorious Caesar (Octavian/Augustus) celebrating his triumph in Rome.

66 *triplici ... triumpho*. A threefold victory because it was celebrated two years later in 29 BC after Augustus consolidated his victory over Antony and Cleopatra by invading Egypt itself (30 BC) as well as winning battles at Illyricum (in 35 and 34 BC, securing the northeast frontier of Italy) and Actium, giving him decisive control over the east.

68 *maxima ... urbem*. Explains the vow of line 67. *ter centum* is used as a large and impressive round number: in his *Res Gestae* (20) Augustus claims to have built or restored 82.

70–71 *omnibus ... iuvencae*. Scenes of ritual public thanksgiving. For the anaphora of *omnibus* cf. lines 57–58.

72 **niveo ... Phoebi**. Augustus' marble temple dedicated to Apollo on the Palatine was not dedicated until October 28 BC, but it is envisaged here because it makes a striking contrast with the simple buildings on the Palatine that Evander shows Aeneas earlier in Book 8. The temple is also referred to in Book 6, where Aeneas promises to dedicate a temple to Apollo (Book 6.69–70).

73–74 aptat ... postibus. Booty from battles was often fixed to the entrances of temples, and this action of Augustus looks back to where Aeneas dedicated a shield at Actium (*Aen.* 3.286 ff.).

74–80 *incedunt ... Araxes*. The accumulation of far-away tribes subdued by Augustus creates a composite picture of the extent of the Roman empire under Augustus and the variety of its peoples. The peoples were previously unconquered (*indomiti*) and even the rivers resentful (*indignatus*) but now Augustus has pacified them, symbolising the completeness of the Pax Augusta.

Lines 81–83

Aeneas' response to the shield.

81 *talia*. Indicates a return to Aeneas from the narrative of the shield.

82 *miratur*. Cf. line 12.

82 *rerum ... gaudet*. *ignarus* is either absolute or to be taken with *rerum*. Either way, the historical events on the shield are pictures for Aeneas.

83 *attollens ... nepotum*. Like Atlas, Aeneas takes on his shoulders not just the shield but the burden of Rome's destiny and history lived out by his successors. In this the episode of the shield in the *Aeneid* is markedly different from the one in the *Iliad* (19.18), where Achilles takes pleasure in the beauty of the shield but there is no element of destiny.

Further teaching suggestions

Content

- What is the relationship between the craftsmanship of the shield and the pictures on it?
- How does Virgil use the shield to bring together Aeneas and Augustus' achievements (see notes above highlighted in **bold italic**)?
- Look at the picture on p. 148. Which of the following details from lines 40–48 are illustrated? *Aegyptia coniunx* (40); *totum ... reductis convulsum remis ... aequor* (41–42); *rostris tridentibus* (42); *turritis puppibus* (45); *stuppea flamma* (46); *volatile ferrum* (46); *sistro* (48).

Style

- 🔊 Listen to the audio CD (tracks 45–48), noticing variations in the rhythm of the metre.
- Comment on the simile in lines 14–16.
- In lines 30–36, see how many corresponding phrases describing Augustus and Agrippa there are and enter them in the table below. One is given as an example.

Augustus	Agrippa
agens Italos	*agmen agens*

- Read aloud lines 56–57. Compare the following translations of lines 56–57. Which do you find most effective in meaning and style?

  (a) But Apollo of Actium saw; and high on his vantage point he already bent his bow. (Knight)

  (b) Viewing all this, Apollo of Actium draws his bow

  From aloft: (Day Lewis)

Further reading

- Fordyce, C. J. (ed.), *Virgil: Aeneid VII–VIII* (Glasgow, Glasgow University Press and Oxford: Oxford University Press, 1977; Bristol Classical Press/Duckworth rev. repr. 1985).

- Gransden, K. W. (ed.), *Virgil: Aeneid Book VIII*, Cambridge Greek and Latin Classics (Cambridge: Cambridge University Press, 1976).

- Knight, W. F. Jackson (trans.), *Virgil: The Aeneid*, Penguin Classics (Harmondworth: Penguin, 1956; rev. repr. 1973).

- Day Lewis, C. (trans.), *Virgil: the Aeneid*, Oxford World's Classics (Oxford: Oxford University Press, 1952; repr. with notes and introduction by J. Griffin, 1986).

- Bradley, P. *Ancient Rome: Using Evidence.* (Edward Arnold (Australia) PTY Ltd 1990. Repr. Cambridge: Cambridge University Press, 2000). Detailed knowledge of the historical background is *not* required for the OCR GCSE in Latin, but this book is useful for reference or for students who wish to pursue questions about the battle of Actium, Octavian/Augustus, and Antony and Cleopatra.